THE DANUBE CYCLEWAY

About the Author

Mike Wells has been a keen cyclist for over 20 years. Starting with UK Sustrans routes, such as Lon Las Cymru in Wales and the C2C route across northern England, he soon moved on to long-distance routes in continental Europe and beyond. These include cycling both the Camino and Ruta de la Plata to Santiago de la Compostela, a traverse of Cuba from end to end, a circumnavigation of Iceland and a trip across Lapland to the North Cape.

This is the third in a series of cycling guides Mike has written for Cicerone, following the great rivers of Europe from their sources. Prior to starting this project he worked in the travel industry organising and escorting tours to many of the places visited in this guide. This enabled him to establish contacts in Vienna, Bratislava and Budapest. In researching this book he cycled the entire route twice, and some parts three times, in order to explore alternative routes on each bank before deciding which was the more attractive to describe in detail.

Other Cicerone guides by the author
Cycling London to Paris
The Adlerweg
The Loire Cycle Route
The Moselle Cycle Route
The Rhine Cycle Route
The River Rhone Cycle Route

THE DANUBE CYCLEWAY

VOLUME 1:
FROM THE SOURCE IN THE BLACK FOREST
TO BUDAPEST

by Mike Wells

JUNIPER HOUSE, MURLEY MOSS,
OXENHOLME ROAD, KENDAL, CUMBRIA LA9 7RL
www.cicerone.co.uk

© Mike Wells 2015
First edition 2015
ISBN: 978 1 85284 722 7
Reprinted 2019 (with updates)

Printed in China on behalf of Latitude Press Ltd

A catalogue record for this book is available from the British Library.
All photographs are by the author unless otherwise stated.

Route mapping by Lovell Johns www.lovelljohns.com
Contains OpenStreetMap.org data © OpenStreetMap
contributors, CC-BY-SA. NASA relief data courtesy of ESRI.

*To Yaz and Cipress at the Cycle Station, who maintain
my bike between long rides across Europe.*

Updates to this Guide

While every effort is made by our authors to ensure the accuracy of guidebooks as they go to print, changes can occur during the lifetime of an edition. Any updates that we know of for this guide will be on the Cicerone
website (www.cicerone.co.uk/722/updates), so please check before planning your trip. We also advise that you check information about such
things as transport, accommodation and shops locally. Even rights of way
can be altered over time. We are always grateful for information about any
discrepancies between a guidebook and the facts on the ground, sent by
email to updates@cicerone.co.uk or by post to Cicerone, Juniper House,
Murley Moss, Oxenholme Road, Kendal LA9 7RL.

Register your book: To sign up to receive free updates, special offers
and GPX files where available, register your book at www.cicerone.co.uk.

Front cover: The Danube Cycleway passes through the middle of Budapest, with
a view of the Hungarian parliament building (Stage 29)

CONTENTS

MAP KEY

🚲	start of route	❶	tourist information
🚲	end of route	■	railway station
🚲	start/finish point	▲	youth hostel
∿	main route	♱	cathedral
∿	alternative route	🏰	castle
→	route direction	✈	airport
➡	alternative route direction	☆	point of interest
	built-up area	⚓	ferry
	forested area	▲	peak
	international border	▲	cave
	regional border		
Route map scale 1:150,000 0 ▬▬ 2 km		✗	battlefield site

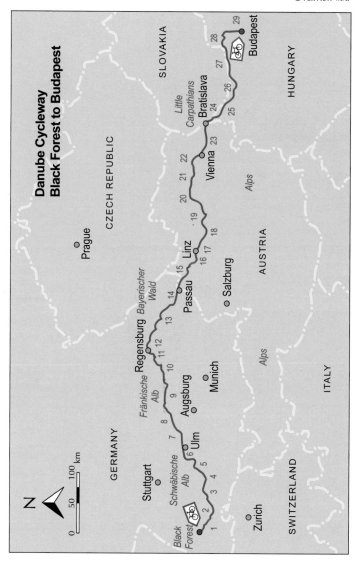

A good cycle track closely follows the Danube
through the bends of Schlögener Schlinge gorge (Stage 15)

INTRODUCTION

A statue of the Roman emperor, Marcus Aurelius, in Tulln (Stage 21)

Everyone has heard the *Blue Danube* by Johann Strauss, the most popular waltz tune ever written and unofficial second Austrian national anthem. The words, which are less well known, tell of 'a bright and blue river, flowing calmly through valley and meadow, ancient castles looking down from on high, past craggy hilltops with mountain views, all the way from the Black Forest through Wien (Vienna) to the sea'. You may be lucky and catch the Danube on a blue day, but most of the time it will appear silvery grey. But do not despair; your trip along the Danube will be filled with many colours, not just blue.

At 2772km, the Danube is Europe's second longest river (behind the Volga). Rising in the German Schwarzwald (Black Forest), only a few metres from the continental watershed, it runs through or past 10 countries on its way to the Black Sea. This guidebook covers the first 1125km of the river from the source to Budapest, taking in the four countries of Germany, Austria, Slovakia and Hungary. On the way you will pass through five different gorges with craggy green treelined cliffs of white limestone rising high above the river. You will pass great abbeys and baroque palaces of the Habsburg rulers often painted in yellow, the favourite colour of Archduchess Maria Theresa. When you arrive in Hungary your taste buds will be assaulted by paprika, the fruit of which blazes red in autumn fields. In the Wachau and around Vienna you will cycle through vineyards producing mostly white wine. But if Black Forest, green trees, white cliffs, yellow palaces, red paprika and white wine are not enough colours for you, the route passes through Blaubeueren. Here, at the blue pool you will find the source of the Blau (Blue) River where naturally occurring chemicals make this small Danube tributary run bright blue.

The great attraction to a cyclist of following a river from its source is that, once you have reached the start, it is almost all downhill. From the easily reached source near Martinskapelle, the Danube Cycleway descends nearly 1000m on its way to Budapest, 1269km distant. The cycling is straightforward with much of the route following well-surfaced cycle tracks, often along the riverbank or flood dykes. On the occasions where roads are used, these are usually quiet country routes. Germany and Austria are extremely cycle-friendly countries, and motorists will generally give you plenty of room. In Slovakia and Hungary cycle infrastructure is less well developed, but rapidly improving. This route is suitable for both experienced long-distance cyclists and those who have not done much cycle touring and wish to start with a straightforward easily followed route.

The route mostly follows part of EuroVelo route 6 (EV6), a trans-continental cycle route running from the Atlantic coast of France to the Black Sea. This is well waymarked in Germany and Austria, slightly less so, but improving, in Slovakia and Hungary. This guide breaks the route into 29 stages, averaging under 44km per stage. A fit cyclist, covering two stages per day, should be able to complete the trip in a fortnight. Allowing three weeks would provide more time for sightseeing and allow the route to be cycled at a leisurely pace. You can break the journey at almost any point as there are many places to stay along the way. These are suitable for all budgets and vary from youth hostels through to B&Bs, guest houses and hotels. If you don't mind the extra weight of camping gear, there are many official campsites.

En route you will pass by some of central Europe's great sights. Soon after leaving Donaueschingen are the Donauversikerung sinkholes, where at times of low water flow the Danube disappears underground allowing you to walk on the dry riverbed. At Sigmaringen the great castle of the Hohenzollerns is still inhabited by a branch of the German royal family. Ulm cathedral has the highest church spire in the world. Before Kelheim and after Regensburg are two huge 19th-century neo-classical monuments built for King Ludwig of Bavaria to celebrate the German nation. The industrial city of Linz was favoured by

Schloss Sigmaringen, ancestral home of the Hohenzollern-Sigmaringen branch of the German imperial family (Stage 3)

Adolf Hitler (it was his birthplace), and the nearby Mauthausen concentration camp memorial is a poignant reminder of the horror of Hitler's time. Great abbeys at Melk and Klosterneuburg echo the connection between Habsburg rulers and Catholic church. The Wachau gorge is Austria's prime wine-producing region. Bratislava and Győr are successful examples of cities recovering rapidly from 40 years of decline under communism. Esztergom is the religious capital of Hungary, while Visegrád castle high above the Danube bend dates from the 13th century.

And of course there are the two great imperial cities of Vienna and Budapest, with their grand thoroughfares, royal palaces, imposing cathedrals, national parliaments, important museums, leading art galleries, opera houses and concert halls. The route described in this guide follows riverside cycle tracks through the centres of both cities. The ride would be worth doing if only to visit them; everything else is a bonus!

BACKGROUND

As the major river of central and south-eastern Europe, the Danube has played a significant role in the history of the continent, first as a border, then as an invasion route and later as an important transport and trade artery.

A Roman frontier
The first civilisation to recognise the importance of the river was the Romans. After pushing north over the Alps, they arrived on the banks of the Danube around 15BC. Seeing

11

the value of a natural and defendable northern border to protect their empire from barbarian tribes, the Romans established fortified settlements along the river from Germany all the way to the Black Sea; the largest of these on the section covered by this guide being Castra Regina (Regensburg), Vindobona (Vienna), Carnuntum (near Hainburg), Brigetio (Komárom) and Aquincum (near Budapest). The border area was known to the Romans as the Limes and settlements were connected by a series of roads. In Germany, the Romans advanced across the Danube as far as the River Main in AD75, but withdrew again in AD263. By the end of the fourth century the Romans were coming under sustained pressure from barbarian tribes from the north and east. Consequently their legions were withdrawn from the Danube frontier around the turn of the fifth century ending over 400 years of Roman rule.

The Holy Roman Empire

After a period of tribal infighting, by AD650 the region had settled into three kingdoms: the Franks controlling the upper Danube (modern-day German territory), Slavic tribes in control of the middle river (modern-day Austria) and Avars (nomadic tribes from central Asia) controlling the Carpathian basin (modern-day Hungary). During the reign of Charlemagne (AD768 to AD814) the Frankish territories were greatly expanded in all directions, including east into the Slavic lands,

which were renamed the Öster Reich (eastern empire) and repopulated with emigrants from Bavaria. In recognition of his power over much of Europe, Charlemagne was crowned Roman Emperor by Pope Leo III in AD800.

After Charlemagne's death, his territories became divided with the eastern part becoming the Holy Roman Empire (HRE), with Otto I (AD972) the first in a line of emperors that was to last until 1806. Although the territories of the HRE extended right across central Europe and down into Italy, the HRE was never a politically unified state. Rather it was a loose confederation of hundreds of principalities, duchies, free imperial cities, bishoprics and other demesnes, the leaders of which (collectively known as 'electors') came together occasionally to elect one of their number as emperor – an early, although very limited, form of democracy. Over time the larger stronger states came to dominate this arrangement and after 1438 the Austrian Habsburg rulers more or less assumed the title of Holy Roman Emperor.

One of the major threats to the unity of the HRE was religious division, the growth of Protestant dissent resulting eventually in the Thirty Years' War (1618–1648), which pitched Catholic states within the HRE against Protestant ones. Neighbouring countries were drawn in; indeed in Württemberg most of the damage was wrought by Swedish troops. By the time of the Peace of

Westphalia, which ended the war, an estimated eight million people had died as a result of fighting, famine, disease and population upheaval. In some towns 75 per cent of the population died and it took almost 100 years for populations to return to pre-war levels. A result was further decline in the central unifying influence and power of the HRE. The French enlightenment philosopher Voltaire (1694–1778) described the Holy Roman Empire as 'neither Holy, nor Roman nor an Empire'.

Hungary and the Magyars

Between AD895 and AD907, the Avars in Hungary were succeeded by another wave of nomadic tribes from central Asia. The Magyars, led by Árpád, settled the country between various tribal groups. In 1000 the conversion to Catholic Christianity of King Istvan I (Stephen I), who was canonised as Szent Istvan, and adoption of western European script and methods of government, established Hungary as a European nation. Over the next 500 years a succession of kings steadily expanded the Hungarian Kingdom and by the beginning of the 16th century it included all of modern-day Slovakia, much of Croatia and parts of Austria, Poland, Serbia, Romania and Ukraine. However, a peasants' revolt in 1514 and disputes between the king and his nobles left the country in a weak position between two other powerful empires, the Ottoman Turks and Austrian Habsburgs.

Ottoman Turks

Constantinople (modern-day Istanbul) was captured by the Islamic Ottoman

The Magyars are celebrated in Budapest Heroes' Square (Stage 29)

The Hofburg palace in Vienna was the centre of Habsburg rule (Stage 22)

Turks in 1453 and over the following decades they continued to move north into the Balkans. In 1525 the Ottomans, who had long held ambitions to extend their territories across the Balkans into central Europe, formed an alliance with France aimed at confronting the power of the Habsburg-dominated Holy Roman Empire. Having taken Belgrade (1521), then a Hungarian city, Turkish forces were well placed to march upon the Habsburg capital Vienna. To do so they had first to conquer Hungary. In 1526 the advancing Turks routed a Hungarian army, commanded by King Ladislaus II, at the Battle of Mohács, and although the king managed to escape he drowned crossing the river. Many Serbs and Hungarians fled before the arrival of the Ottomans who captured Budapest

unopposed and went on to lay siege to Vienna in 1529, but they failed to capture it. The death of Ladislaus, who had no heir, marked the end of the independent Hungarian Kingdom, the crown passing by marriage to the Austrian Habsburgs, who ruled what was left of the country from Pressburg (modern-day Bratislava).

For nearly 160 years the Ottoman Turks controlled the Hungarian Danube basin, ruling over a mainly empty land, the Christian population having either fled or been slaughtered. A number of attempts to push further into western Europe were unsuccessful, culminating in defeat at the second siege of Vienna (1683) a battle that was hailed by the Catholic church as the final victory of Christianity over Islam in Europe. The Ottoman Turks were gradually pushed back through

Hungary by Habsburg forces, before being expelled altogether after the Battle of Belgrade (1688).

The Habsburgs

The House of Habsburg, which originated in 11th-century Switzerland, came to prominence when Rudolf von Habsburg became king of Germany (1273) and Duke of Austria (1282). After becoming the dominant force in the HRE, a series of dynastic marriages expanded Habsburg power over Spain and its American colonies, Burgundy, the Netherlands, Bohemia and much of Italy. Along the Danube they controlled Austria itself, the Austrian Vorland (modern Württemberg) and Slovakia after 1526. When Prince Eugene of Savoy, commanding Habsburg forces, drove Turkish forces out of Hungary

in 1688, Hungary and its territories in Croatia, Serbia and Transylvania all came under Habsburg rule. The Danube was the major transport corridor linking this empire together and there are many towns along the river that can claim 'the emperor stayed here'. After the death of Archduke Charles VI (1740), his daughter Maria Theresa became Archduchess and her husband, Francis Stephan, Holy Roman Emperor. Many of the great imperial buildings of the region date from this period including Schönbrunn palace in Vienna.

Napoleon Bonaparte

Despite ruling France for only 16 years, Napoleon (1769–1821) had a greater influence on the political and legal structures of Europe than any

Befreiungshalle above Kelheim was built to commemorate German liberation from Napoleon (Stage 10)

other person. Rising to power after the disruptions of the French Revolution, a series of military campaigns saw Napoleon gain control of much of western and central Europe. After defeating Austrian and Russian forces at Austerlitz (1805) he forced Austria to surrender and took control of the Habsburg territories. Napoleon is often credited with redrawing the map of Europe. By sweeping away the multiplicity of small states that formed the HRE, he effectively ended the Empire. Germany was reorganised into 40 states making up the Confederation of the Rhine, while the territories of the Austrian Vorland were amalgamated with neighbouring states into the Duchy of Baden. Only Bavaria, an ally of France, maintained its independence. Perhaps the longest lasting of Napoleonic reforms was the Code Napoleon, a civil legal code that was adopted throughout the conquered territories and remains today at the heart of the European legal system. When he was defeated in 1814 and 1815 by the combined forces of the UK, Russia, Austria and Prussia, the latter was one of two German states that emerged in a strong position (the other was Bavaria). These two states stepped into the void created by the end of the HRE, with the Bavarians extending their territory across much of southern Germany.

Two Great Empires

Following the fall of Napoleon, the Habsburgs strengthened their control over Austria and Hungary. In 1848 a violent uprising seeking Hungarian independence was put down by Austria and Russia. However, Hungary did gain a measure of self-government under the overall rule of the emperor, with the Habsburg possessions being restructured in 1867 as the Austro-Hungarian Empire. In Germany, Prussia (which had never been part of the HRE) emerged as the dominant force under 'Iron Chancellor' Bismarck and, after merging with Bavaria following the defeat of France in the Franco-Prussian War (1870–1871), it became the Deutsches Reich (German Empire).

These two empires both had strong militaristic tendencies and, following unrest in the Balkans, they allied themselves against the UK, France and Russia. The First World War (1914–1918), fought between these two alliances, resulted in little or no action in the upper Danube basin, most of the military conflict being in France, Russia, Italy and Turkey.

The Treaty of Versailles and its consequences

The Treaty of Versailles (with Germany), Treaty of St Germain (with Austria) and the Trianon Treaty (with Hungary), which ended the war, had an enormous effect on both Austria-Hungary and Germany. The Habsburgs lost their throne after over 600 years of rule and the Austro-Hungarian Empire was dismantled, with Romania and the new countries of Yugoslavia and Czechoslovakia taking much of its

The gates that once marked the Iron Curtain are nowadays permanently open (Stage 23)

territory. In Germany the effect was mostly economic, large reparation payments leading to national bankruptcy and political unrest. The Nazi party, founded in Bavaria and led by Adolf Hitler, took advantage of this upheaval, taking power in Germany in 1933 with a policy that included overturning Versailles and expanding German territory. A referendum in Austria (1938) led to the *anschluss* (political union) between Germany and Austria under Nazi control. German invasions of Czechoslovakia and Poland led to the Second World War (1939–1945), with Hungary, seeking to regain territory lost in Trianon, joining the German-Austrian Axis. During the war, Nazi anti-semitic actions led to the enslavement or slaughter of six million Jews in concentration camps including that at Mauthausen.

The Iron Curtain and communism

Defeat in the war led to the Danube basin coming under the control of the victorious Allied powers, with Baden-Württemberg occupied by France, Bavaria and Oberösterreich by the US and Niederösterreich, Czechoslovakia and Hungary by soviet Russia. While the West German and Austrian states soon regained independent nationhood, Czechoslovakia and Hungary remained under soviet control. Communist governments were imposed with private property expropriated by the state and farming collectivised. The border between soviet-controlled eastern Europe and western Europe was heavily fortified by Russia with a line of defences described by Winston Churchill as an 'iron curtain' (crossed on Stage 23). Despite uprisings in Hungary (1956) and

Czechoslovakia (1968), neither country obtained independence until 1989.

European Union

Germany was one of the original signatories to the Treaty of Rome (1957), which established the European Economic Community (EEC) and led to the European Union (EU). Austria acceded to the treaty in 1995 with both Slovakia (which had seceded from Czechoslovakia in 1993) and Hungary joining in 2004. All four countries have also signed the Schengen agreement allowing barrier-free trade and travel within the Schengen zone. As a result there are now no border controls anywhere along the route. Both Austria and Germany were founder members of the Eurozone currency union, with the economic success of Slovakia since independence allowing it to join in 2009. Although Austria, Germany and Slovakia appear wedded to the European project, in Hungary there is a strong nationalistic movement that dreams unrealistically of returning the country to the pre-Trianon borders of Greater Hungary.

As history has shown, this is not the first time that the whole of the upper and middle Danube has been politically unified. The Romans, Habsburgs and Nazis all forced unity upon the region; this time unity has been achieved by democratic means!

Shipping on the river

The Danube is a major trade artery. Partially navigable below Ulm, the river becomes a major navigation after being joined by the Rhein–Main–Donau canal at Kelheim. This enables

Luxury cruise boats sail mainly between Passau and Budapest

Kloster Weltenburg Abbey stands at the entrance of Donaudurchbruch gorge (Stage 10)

large barges to cross Europe from the North Sea to the Black Sea. Tourist boats, a very popular way of seeing the river, mostly cruise between Passau and Budapest, although some go all the way from Amsterdam to the Black Sea. Navigation on the river is controlled by an international commission. Large number boards appear beside the river at regular intervals below Ulm showing the distance in kilometres from the Black Sea.

NATURAL ENVIRONMENT

Physical geography

The course of the Danube above Budapest has been greatly influenced by geomorphic events further south approximately 30 million years ago, when the Alps and Carpathians were pushed up by the collision of the African and European tectonic plates. This caused rippling of the landmass to the north, creating successive ridges that form the limestone mountains of Schwarzwald, Schwäbische Alb, Fränkische Alb and Bayerischer Wald. Through Germany and Austria, the river follows the northern edge of the Bavarian pre-Alpen plateau, passing between this plateau and higher ground to the north formed by these successive ridges. En route it cuts through a number of outliers from the main ridges and here the Danube has created gorges through the limestone rock. These formations are particularly evident through the Schwäbische Alb (Stage 3), through the Fränkische Alb between Weltenburg and Kelheim (Stage 9), through the edge of the Bayerischer Wald below Passau (Stage

19

15) and again between Grein and Krems (Stages 19–20). At Hainburg, between Vienna and Bratislava (Stage 23), the Danube cuts through a gap between the eastern extremity of the Alps and the Little Carpathian Mountains. Beyond Bratislava the river crosses the sandy basin of the Little Danube Plain, then cuts another gorge through an outlier of the Little Carpathians before reaching the Great Hungarian Plain at Budapest.

Prior to the end of the last Ice Age (14,000 years ago), the Danube was a longer and even greater river. The upper waters of the Rhine, which rise in the High Alps of central Switzerland and flow down through Bodensee, originally flowed north from this lake to join the Danube above Ulm. A connection between the river basins of these two rivers still exists, although now it operates in the opposite direction, where sinkholes (*versickerung*) in the Danube near Immendingen (Stage 2) and Fridingen (Stage 3) channel water underground from the Danube south to Bodensee and so into the Rhine. The proportion of Danube water flowing through these sinkholes is steadily increasing and eventually the upper Danube above Sigmaringen will be completely captured by the Rhine.

The Danube is fed by a number of important tributaries, including the Lech, Isar and Inn that rise on the northern side of the Alps. These are fed by glacial meltwaters and spring snow-melt that bring milky water containing ground up quartz and suspended limestone down to the Danube. This is particularly evident at Passau where the milky water of the Inn and clearer Danube water run side by side for some distance before eventually blending together. Much of this suspension is deposited as sediment when the river reaches the flat lands of the Hungarian Plain. The short Blau River, which rises in the Schwäbische Alb at Blaubueren and joins the Danube at Ulm (Stage 6), has a chemical impurity that makes its water appear blue.

Wildlife

While a number of small mammals (including rabbits, hares, red squirrels, voles, water rats and weasels) may be seen scuttling across the track and deer glimpsed in forests, this is not a route inhabited by rare animals, with one exception. After nearly becoming extinct through hunting, the European beaver has been successfully reintroduced to various places along the Danube in Germany and Austria. Inhabiting riparian wooded wetlands, the beaver fells small trees by gnawing through their trunks to create dammed areas of fresh water, within which they build their characteristic lodges. As they are mainly nocturnal, your chances of seeing a beaver are slight, although you may spot one of their lodges.

However, there is a wide range of interesting birdlife. White swans, geese and many varieties of ducks inhabit the river and its banks.

A tree felled by beavers in Mülheim Nature Reserve to create a dam (Stage 3)

A storks' nest atop Heilig-Kreuz abbey in Donauwörth (Stage 8)

Cruising above, raptors, particularly buzzards and kites, are frequently seen hunting small mammals. Birds that live by fishing include cormorants, noticeable when perched on rocks with their wings spread out to dry, and kingfishers. These exist in many locations, mostly on backwaters, perching where they can observe the water. Despite their bright blue and orange plumage they are very difficult to spot. Grey herons, on the other hand, are very visible. Common all along this part of the Danube, they can be seen standing in shallow water waiting to strike or stalking purposefully along the banks.

Perhaps the most noticeable birds are white storks. These huge birds, with a wingspan of two metres, nest in trees or on man-made platforms. They feed on small mammals and reptiles, which they catch in water meadows or on short grassland. Stork numbers in central Europe declined during the 20th century but conservation programmes have led to a significant growth in population and white storks are no longer regarded as a threatened species.

Among a wide variety of reptiles, such as lizards, newts and snakes, perhaps the most exotic are European pond terrapins. These small turtles can be found in a number of locations, including the warm springs near Algershofen (Stage 5) and Schloss Orth castle in the Donau-Auen national park (Stage 23).

A European pond terrapin in Donau-Auen national park (Stage 23)

THE ROUTE

The 1269km Danube Cycleway passes through four countries, with the first 630km in Germany through the *lander* (states) of Baden-Württemberg and Bavaria. This is followed by 379km across Austria through the states of Oberösterreich and Niederösterreich. A short 24km section in Slovakia is followed by a 236km stretch through Hungary to reach Budapest.

Germany

The route starts at the source of the Danube's longest tributary, the Breg, which rises high in the German Black Forest near the small hamlet of Martinskapelle, just a few metres from the great European watershed that divides rivers flowing north and west into the Atlantic from those flowing south and east into the Mediterranean. A few kilometres downstream is the start of a dedicated cycle track that runs along the route of an old railway through Bregtal to Donaueschingen, a town that claims to be the start of the Danube. Here the Breg is joined by the Brigach; the combined river is known as the Donau.

For the next 160km (Stages 2–5) the Donauradweg heads northeast, passing below the southern edge of the Schwäbische Alb mountains through a series of attractive Württemberg towns. A scenic route briefly away from the river (Stage 6) is followed through Blautal to reach Ulm, the first city on the Danube. Still heading north-east, but now in Bavaria, along the northern edge of the Bavarian plateau (Stages 7–9) the route goes through prosperous towns such as Ingolstadt (home of Audi), which ooze both history and modern-day Bavarian economic success.

Cutting through the edge of the Fränkische Alb mountains (Stages 10–11) by way of the Donaudurchbruch gorge between Weltenburg and Kelheim, the next big city reached is Regensburg. The route (Stages 12–14) now changes direction to head south-east closely following the river below the thickly wooded mountains of the Bayerischer Wald (Bavarian Forest, a part of the Bohemian massif) before reaching Passau, the last town in Germany on the Danube.

Austria

After entering Austria on Donau-radweg R1 the route continues south-east (Stages 15–16) through the Schlögener Schlinge gorge between the Bayerischer Wald and Sauwald mountains to reach Linz an industrial city, the third largest in Austria. Still following the edge of the Bohemian Massif (Stages 17–19), the route passes Mauthausen, where the site of Austria's largest Second World War concentration camp is now a memorial to those who died in the atrocities, and Melk with its great Benedictine abbey standing high above the river. The next section (Stages 20–22) passes through the Wachau, Austria's principal wine-producing region, before reaching Vienna, the Austrian capital and one of Europe's great cultural cities. The final stage in Austria (Stage 23) goes through the Donau-Auen national park and the Hainburg Gap between the Alps and Carpathian Mountains, a place that marks the end

The limestone cliffs of Donautal gorge where the Danube cuts through the Schwäbische Alb mountains (Stage 3)

23

of western Europe and the beginning of eastern Europe.

Slovakia and Hungary

The trip through eastern Europe (Stages 24–29) starts with the Slovak capital Bratislava, a city that is rapidly shrugging off the economic problems of the former communist era, and then follows the Mosoni Duna River across the Little Hungarian Plain to Győr, another post-communist success story. After rejoining the Danube at Komárom, the cathedral city of Esztergom and the castle of Visegrad overlooking the picturesque Danube Bend are visited en route to Budapest, the Hungarian capital. If you want to carry on following the Danube, it is 1718km by cycle from Budapest to the Black Sea; but that's another story.

When to go

The route is generally cyclable from April to October. Indeed, much of the route can be cycled at any time of year except for the Black Forest section (Stage 1) where snow can lie until April, see Safety and emergencies for further information.

The tourist season tends to run from 1 May until 30 September. This is particularly noticeable in Austria where many ferries and attractions are closed or operate restricted hours outside this period. During July and August (the school holiday season) the route can become very busy. However, there is such a wide variety of accommodation available it is seldom difficult to find somewhere to stay.

Average temperatures (max/min degrees C)							
	Apr	May	Jun	Jul	Aug	Sep	Oct
Black Forest	10/1	16/6	18/9	21/11	23/11	17/8	12/4
Regensburg	14/3	20/8	23/11	24/12	24/12	19/8	13/4
Vienna	15/6	21/11	23/14	26/15	25/15	20/12	14/7
Budapest	16/6	21/11	24/14	27/15	26/15	22/15	16/7

Average rainfall (mm/rainy days)							
	Apr	May	Jun	Jul	Aug	Sep	Oct
Black Forest	39/15	61/15	57/16	60/15	56/16	56/16	58/18
Regensburg	24/10	47/11	78/10	57/11	70/9	40/9	35/10
Vienna	52/8	62/9	70/9	68/9	58/8	54/7	40/6
Budapest	47/6	65/8	70/8	50/7	50/6	43/5	47/5

The journey ends under Széchenyi chain bridge in Budapest (Stage 29)

How long will it take?

The main route has been broken into 29 stages averaging 44km per stage. A fit cyclist, cycling an average of 90km per day should be able to complete the route in a fortnight. Travelling at a gentler pace of 60km per day and allowing time for sightseeing, cycling the Danube to Budapest would take three weeks. There are many places to stay all along the route and it is easy to tailor daily distances to your requirements. You could of course continue all the way to the Black Sea, which would take a fit cyclist three more weeks. A very fit cyclist could do the whole journey from Black Forest to Black Sea in an energetic month in the saddle.

What kind of cycle is suitable?

Most of the route through Austria and Slovakia is on asphalt cycle tracks or alongside quiet country roads. There are some stretches with gravel surfaces, particulary in Germany, but these are invariably well graded and pose few problems for most kinds of bicycle. In Hungary there are some short sections using unmade dirt tracks that can become muddy and difficult after flooding or heavy rain. As a result, cycling the exact route as described in this guide is not recommended for narrow-tyred racing cycles. There are, however, on-road alternatives for these stages, which can be used to bypass the rougher sections. The most suitable type of cycle is either a touring cycle or a hybrid (a lightweight but strong cross between a touring cycle and a mountain bike with at least 21 gears). There is no advantage in using a mountain bike.

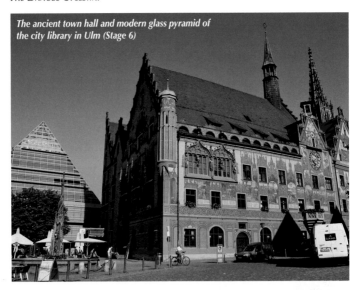

The ancient town hall and modern glass pyramid of the city library in Ulm (Stage 6)

Front suspension is beneficial as it absorbs much of the vibration. Straight handlebars, with bar-ends enabling you to vary your position regularly, are recommended. Make sure your cycle is serviced and lubricated before you start, particularly the brakes, gears and chain.

As important as the cycle is your choice of tyres. Slick road tyres are not suitable and knobbly mountain bike tyres not necessary. What you need is something in-between with good tread and a slightly wider profile than you would use for everyday cycling at home. To reduce the chance of punctures, choose tyres with puncture-resistant armouring, such as a Kevlar™ band.

GETTING THERE AND BACK

By rail

The start of the route in the Black Forest (altitude 1094m) is not directly accessible by train. However, Triberg station (617m) is only 12km of fairly easy ascent from the source. Triberg is on the highly scenic Schwarzwaldbahn railway line that runs from north to south through the Black Forest between Offenburg and Singen via Donaueschingen with hourly trains that carry cycles. It can be reached by connections across the DB (German railway) network.

If travelling from the UK, you can take your cycle on Eurostar from London St Pancras (not Ebbsfleet nor

Ashford) to Brussels (Midi). Trains to Brussels run approximately two-hourly throughout the day. Cycles booked in advance travel in dedicated cycle spaces in the baggage compartment of the same train as you. Bookings, which open six months in advance and cost £30 single, should be made through Eurostar baggage (tel 0844 822 5822). Cycles must be checked-in at the Eurostar baggage office (beside the bus dropping-off point at the back of the station) at least one hour before departure. There are two dedicated spaces per train for fully assembled cycles and four more for disassembled cycles

packed in a special fibre glass case. These cases are provided by Eurostar at the despatch counter, along with tools and packing advice. Leave yourself plenty of time to dismantle and pack your bike. If no space is available your cycle can be sent as registered luggage (£25) and is guaranteed to arrive within 24hr. More information can be found at www.eurostar.com.

After Brussels the route becomes more complicated as the high-speed Thalys and ICE trains that provide a regular connection with Germany take folding cycles or cycles only with their front wheels removed and packed

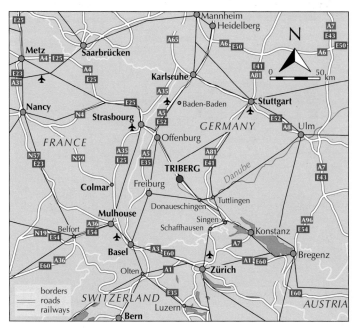

The 16th-century Schöne Stiege with its outside staircase is now the town museum in Riedlingen (Stage 4)

in a carrier no bigger than 1200mm x 900mm. If you want to avoid dismantling your bike, there is an hourly regional service to Welkenraedt for a connection via Aachen to Köln from where two more regional trains will take you via Mainz and Karlsruhe to Triberg. For the Belgian part of the journey to Welkenraedt you are required to purchase a one-day cycle ticket but once in Germany your bike goes free, although if you use IC (intercity) trains you will need to make a reservation. Leaving London around 08.00 will enable you to reach Triberg by 22.00. To plan this journey using only bicycle-permitted trains, go to the German railways website www.bahn. com. Enter your intended journey then click-on 'further details' and select 'carriage of bicycle'. This can all be done in English.

It is possible (and much faster) to travel to Paris (Gare du Nord) by Eurostar then continue from Paris (Gare de l'Est) to Strasbourg using TGV high speed trains (Gare de l'Est is a 5min ride from Gare du Nord). However, the TGV Est trains that operate this service do not carry fully assembled cycles so this option is viable only if you are prepared to disassemble and pack your bike in a 1200mm x 900mm carrier. The good news is that a packed cycle counts as carry-on hand luggage and incurs no charges. From Strasbourg, regional DB trains can be used to reach Offenburg and continue to Triberg. Details of French trains and booking can be found at www.oui.sncf. Up to date information on travelling by train with a bicycle can be found on a website dedicated to worldwide rail travel, 'The man in seat 61', www.seat61. com.

By air

Airports at Basel/Freiburg/Mulhouse, Strasbourg, Karlsruhe/Baden, Stuttgart and Zürich can be used to access the Danube source. None is particularly close, all being between two and three hours by train from Triberg. Airlines have different requirements regarding how cycles are presented and some, but not all, make a charge, which you should pay when booking as it is usually greater at the airport. All require tyres partially deflated, handlebars turned and pedals removed (loosen pedals beforehand to make them easier to remove at the airport). Most will accept your cycle in a transparent polythene bike-bag, although some insist on use of a cardboard bike-box. These can be obtained from cycle shops, usually for free. You do, however, have the problem of how you get the box to the airport.

By road

If you are lucky enough to have someone prepared to drive you to the start, Martinskapelle is a short distance from the B500 (Black Forest Panoramaweg), south-west of Triberg. With your own vehicle the most convenient places to leave it are Karlsruhe or Stuttgart, from where trains can be used to reach Triberg on the outward journey and which can be reached within a day by train from Budapest on the return (see below). If driving from England, Stuttgart is between 750km and 800km from the Channel ports, depending upon route.

European Bike Express operates a coach service with dedicated cycle trailer from northern England, picking up en route across England to the Mediterranean, with a drop-off point at Nancy in eastern France. Go to www.bike-express.co.uk for details and bookings. Trains link Nancy to Strasbourg with connections on to Offenburg and Triberg.

Intermediate access

There are international airports at Linz, Vienna and Bratislava. By train, Stuttgart airport is accessible from Ulm and Munich airport from Ingolstadt. Much of the route is closely followed by railway lines; stations en route are listed in the text.

Onward travel

Budapest has two stations served by international trains, Keleti (eastern) (services to Vienna, Munich and western Germany) and Nyugati (western) stations (trains for the airport, as well as services to Bratislava, Prague and Berlin). Unfortunately the high-speed ÖBB (Austrian) Railjet trains that link Keleti with Vienna and Munich every two hours do not carry bicycles. To reach Vienna it is necessary to catch a series of regional trains either from Budapest Deli via Győr or from Nyugati via Bratislava. From Vienna, international trains with bicycle accommodation (excluding Railjet and ICE high-speed trains) run to stations all over Europe. If returning to collect a car left near the start, trains

The Hungarian Parliament building stands beside the Danube in Budapest (Stage 29)

FERIHEGY STATION TO BUDAPEST AIRPORT, TERMINAL 2

From Feriheghy station, it is a 6km ride to terminal 2. Turn R outside the entrance to Ferihegy station (do not cross the motorway into the airport) and follow a good cycle track alongside the motorway to reach a large out of town shopping centre at Vecsés. Opposite a Shell petrol station, turn L across the main road and immediately L again on a short track that continues across the highway to a bus stop on the opposite side. Turn L and follow this track over a grass bank beneath an advertising sign. Turn R onto a quiet road and continue through trees to reach the old airport perimeter road. Turn R then bear L parallel to the highway. Just before this road emerges onto the highway, turn L onto a road serving a small aviation museum. Just before the museum entrance turn R on a block track, which leads past airport car parks L to reach terminal 2.

via Salzburg and Munich allow you to reach Stuttgart or Karlsruhe in one day from Budapest.

The most direct routes for those bound for the UK involve using DB (German) ICE trains from Stuttgart to Paris or ICE and Thalys trains from Frankfurt to Brussels via Köln, then Eurostar to London. Neither of these options take fully assembled cycles and you would need to disassemble your bike and pack in a 1200mm x 900mm carrier. If do not want to disassemble your bike, the only option is to use DB IC trains to reach Köln, then regional trains via Aachen and Welkenraedt to reach Brussels. If you are travelling to northern or eastern Britain another option is to travel from Köln to Venlo (Netherlands) and on to Rotterdam and Hoek van Holland, from where Stena Line (www.stenaline.co.uk) runs two ferries daily (afternoon and overnight) to Harwich. On overnight sailings, passengers must reserve cabins. From

Harwich, trains with cycle provision run to London (Liverpool Street) and to Cambridge, where connections to the rest of the UK can be made. In addition, P&O ferries (www.poferries.com) sail every night from Rotterdam (Europoort) to Hull.

Budapest airport, 18km southeast of the city, has flights to European and worldwide destinations. Trains that carry cycles run every 30 minutes from Nyugati to Ferihegy airport station, which is adjacent to Budapest airport terminal 1. Unfortunately this terminal is closed and all flights leave from terminal 2 on the other side of the airfield. Getting there by cycle is a challenge (see above).

NAVIGATION

Waymarking

With the exception of Stage 1 above Donaueschingen, which mostly uses

Above (left to right): *Bregtalweg waymark; German Donau Radweg waymark in Baden-Württemburg; German Donau-Radwanderweg waymark in Bavaria*
Below (left to right): *Austrian R1 waymark in Oberösterreich; Austrian Donauradweg EV6 waymark in Niederösterreich; Slovak Dunajská Cesta waymark; Hungarian EV6 waymark*

the Bregtalweg, the whole route described follows a series of national waymarked cycle routes. These all carry names incorporating some form of words describing Danube cycleway, in the appropriate language. In addition, from Tuttlingen (Stage 3) all the way to Budapest, the Danube is joined by EuroVelo route EV6, which runs from the Atlantic coast of France to the Black Sea. Germany has allocated D6 to the Danube route within their national system of long-distance cycle routes. In Austria, the route was originally signed throughout as R1 and these waymarks are still used in Oberösterreich (Stages

Summary of cycle routes followed			
	Bregtalweg	Stage 1	Germany (Baden-Württemberg)
EV6	EuroVelo Route 6	Stages 3–29	Germany/Austria/Slovakia/Hungary
	Deutsches Donau	Stages 2–14	Germany
D6	Donau Radweg	Stages 2–14	Germany
AD9	Albdonaukreis 9	Stage 6	Germany (Baden-Württemberg)
	Donau-Radwanderweg	Stages 7–14	Germany (Bavaria)
R1	Donauradweg	Stages 15–17	Austria (Oberösterreich)
	Donaukanalradweg	Stage 22	Austria (Vienna)
	Dunajská Cesta	Stages 23–24	Slovakia

15–17). However, in Niederösterreich (Stages 18–23) signing has been changed and waymarking is now EV6. As the river widens, waymarked cycle routes can often be found on both banks, giving a variety of alternative routes. Although the style of waymarking varies slightly from country to country and stage to stage, the long-term objective is to sign the route throughout (except Stages 1–2) as EV6. In Germany and Austria, waymarking is almost perfect in its consistency, less so in Slovakia and Hungary, but even here the situation has improved in recent years. In the introduction to each stage an indication is given of the predominant waymarks followed.

Maps

Freytag & Berndt, Kompass, Public Press and ADFC all publish maps covering most of the route shown in this book. These vary in scale from 1:50,000 to 1:125,000. The only map that includes Stage 1 (Martinskapelle to Donaueschingen) is Kompass RWK 150.

Various online maps are available to download, at a scale of your choice. Particularly useful is Open Street Map (www.openstreetmap.org), which has a cycle route option showing the route of EV6 in its entirety.

Guidebooks

Esterbauer Bikeline publish a series of three Radtourenbuch und Karte (cycle tour guidebook with maps) in both English and German, covering the route from Donaueschingen to Budapest with strip maps at 1:75,000.

Most of these maps and guidebooks are available from leading bookshops including Stanford's, London and The Map Shop, Upton upon Severn. Relevant maps are widely available en route.

Freytag & Berndt		
1 RK	Donauradweg	1:125,000
Kompass		
RWK 150	Donauradweg Schwarzwald (source) to Regensburg	1:125,000 (map)
RWK 151	Donauradweg Regensburg to Bratislava	1:125,000 (map)
FTK 7009	Donauradweg 1 Donaueschingen to Passau	1:50,000 (cards)
FTK 7004	Donauradweg 2 Passau to Bratislava	1:50,000 (cards)
Public Press		
235	Donauradweg Donaueschingen to Passau	1:50,000
246	Donauradweg Passau to Vienna	1:50,000
ADFC		
EuroVelo 6	Rhine and Danube cycle trail Basel to Budapest	1:100,000 (seven-map set)

ACCOMMODATION

Hotels, inns, guest houses and bed & breakfast

For most of the route there is a wide variety of accommodation. The stage descriptions identify places known to have accommodation, but are by no means exhaustive. Hotels vary from expensive five star properties to modest local establishments. Hotels and inns usually offer a full meal service, guest houses do sometimes. Bed and Breakfasts, which can be recognised by a sign *zimmer frei* ('room available'), generally offer only breakfast. In Hungary best value is often found in a *panzió* (pension). Tourist information offices will often telephone on your behalf and make local reservations. After hours, some tourist offices display a sign outside showing local establishments with vacancies. Booking ahead is seldom

German bett+bike sign

necessary, except on popular stages in high season; however, it is advisable to start looking for accommodation after 1600. In Germany and Austria most hotels and guest houses are closed one night per week, known as *ruhetag* (closed day). If you are planning to stay in a location with only one place to stay, it is worth checking out in advance if ruhetag will affect your plans. Most properties are cycle-friendly and will find you a secure overnight place for your pride and joy.

Prices for accommodation in both Germany and Austria are similar to, or slightly cheaper than, prices in the UK. Slovakia and Hungary are significantly cheaper.

Bett+Bike

Bett+Bike (www.bettundbike.de) is a German scheme run by ADFC (German cycling club), which has registered over 5000 establishments providing cycle-friendly accommodation. It includes a wide variety of properties from major hotels to local B&Bs, listed by state in an annually updated guidebook. Participating establishments display a Bett+Bike sign.

Youth hostels

There are 25 official youth hostels, some in historic buildings, on or near the route (12 German, six Austrian and seven in Budapest), as well as four independent hostels in Bratislava. These are listed in Appendix F. To use a youth hostel you need to be a member of an association affiliated to Hostelling International. If you are not a member you will be required to join the local association. Rules vary from country to country but generally all hostels accept guests of any age, although visitors over 27 may face a small surcharge (€3 in Germany). Rooms vary from single sex dormitories to family rooms of two to six beds. Most continental European hostels do not have self-catering facilities but do provide good value hot meals. Hostels get very busy, particularly during school holidays, and booking is advised through www.hihostels.com.

Camping

If you are prepared to carry camping equipment, this may appear the cheapest way of cycling the Danube. However, good-quality campsites with all facilities are often only a little cheaper than B&Bs or hostels. The stage descriptions identify many official campsites but these are by no means exhaustive. Camping may be possible in other locations with the permission of local landowners.

FOOD AND DRINK

Where to eat

There are thousands of places where cyclists can eat and drink, varying from snack bars, hotdog stands and local inns to Michelin starred restaurants. Locations of many places to eat are listed in stage descriptions, but these are by no means exhaustive. Days and times of opening vary. When planning your day, try to be

The fountain in Ehingen Marktplatz (Stage 5)

flexible as a number of inns and small restaurants do not open at lunchtime and may have one day a week when they remain closed. A local inn offering food and drink is typically known as *gaststätte* in Germany. *Weinstube* is a winebar, often attached to a vineyard. In Hungary an *étterem* is a restaurant. English language menus are often available in big cities and tourist areas, but are less common in smaller towns and rural locations.

When to eat

Breakfast (German *frühstück*; Hungarian *reggeli*) is usually continental; it normally consists of breads, jam and a hot drink with the optional addition of cold meats, cheese and a boiled egg. Traditionally lunch (German *mittagessen*, Hungarian *ebéd*) was the main meal of the day,

but this is slowly changing, and is likely to prove unsuitable if you plan an afternoon in the saddle. The most common lunchtime snacks everywhere are soups and ham or cheese sandwiches. In Germany and Austria it is common for people to consume cakes mid-morning or mid-afternoon, often accompanied by coffee.

For dinner (German *abendessen*, Hungarian *vacsora*) a wide variety of cuisine is available. Portions tend to be large, particularly in Germany. Much of what is available is pan-European and will be easily recognisable. There are, however, national and regional dishes you may wish to try.

What to eat

Germany is the land of the *schwein* (pig) and pork, gammon, bacon and ham dishes dominate German menus.

A German farmers' mixed pork plate with libation

White asparagus is popular in Germany during Spargelzeit between April and June

Traditionally pork was pot-roasted or grilled rather than fried. There are over 1500 types of German *wurst* (sausage), the most common being *bratwurst* (made from minced pork and served grilled or fried), *wienerwurst* (smoked sausages served boiled, known as frankfurters in English) and *weisswurst* (a Bavarian speciality made of pork and veal, served boiled). *Wurst mit senf und brot* (sausages with mustard and bread) and *wurst salat* (thin strips of slicing sausage served with *sauerkraut* (pickled cabbage) are popular lunchtime snacks. *Sauerbraten* is marinated roast beef, while *fleischkaese* and *leberkaese* are kinds of meat loaf. *Forelle* (trout) and *lachs* (salmon) are the most popular fish. The most common vegetable accompaniments are sauerkraut and boiled potatoes. *Reibekuchen* are potato pancakes, served with apple sauce. *Spargel* (white asparagus) is consumed in huge quantities during Spargelzeit between mid-April and 24 June. The most famous German cake is *Schwarzwalder Kirschtorte* (Black Forest gateau), a chocolate and cherry cake.

Austrian cooking is also heavily based on pig meat, but there are some specialities. *Wiener schnitzel* (veal escalope fried in egg and breadcrumbs) is ubiquitous. *Tafelspitz* is braised beef and *gröstl* is a hash made from leftover cooked pork, diced potatoes and onions fried in butter and served with a fried egg. Accompaniments include *knödel* (dense tennis ball size dumplings, *kartoffel* (potatoes) or *spätzle* (noodles). The most common dessert is strudel, usually apple but sometimes *marillen* (apricot), *mohn* (poppy seed) or *topfen* (curd cheese). Other desserts

37

include *Germknödel*, a substantial sweet dumpling served with poppy seeds, plum jam and custard, and *kaiserschmarn*, a pancake made with raisins, which is chopped and served with sugar. A typical Austrian snack, served from mid-morning to mid-afternoon is a *brettjause*, a wooden platter of cold meats, cheese and bread rather like a ploughman's lunch. The most popular cakes include *Sachertorte*, a chocolate and apricot creation that originated in the Hotel Sacher in Vienna.

Despite being most well-known for cooking that uses ample quantities of paprika (mild red pepper), Hungarian cuisine generally offers greater variety than German. Goulash (boiled beef and vegetables, flavoured with paprika) is the national dish and appears on most menus as both a soup (*gulyásleves*) and a main course stew (*székelgulyás*). Paprika is also a key ingredient in chicken paprika (*csirkepaprikás*), a casserole of chicken and vegetables thickened with sour cream. Roast goose is a favourite dish for celebrations. Stuffed cabbage (*töltött káposzta*) and stuffed peppers (*töltött paprika*) are both borrowed from Ottoman cuisine. Pancakes (*palascinta*) can be either savoury (such as *hortobágyi palacsinta*, filled with veal stew) or sweet with jam, chocolate sauce or cream cheese. *Lángos*, a popular street snack, are flat portions of dough fried in oil and served with savoury toppings such as cheese, ham, spicy sausage or mushrooms.

What to drink

Although Germany produces substantial quantities of wine, the part of the country through which the Danube flows, particularly Bavaria, is overwhelmingly a beer producing

Kloster Barrock dunkel dark beer is brewed at Kloster Weltenburg Abbey (Stage 10)

and consuming region. In Germany, purity laws controlling the production and content of beer have limited the mass consolidation of brewing compared to other European countries, beer still being brewed in a large number of local breweries. *Pilsener*, a pale lager, is the most widely drunk form, although *weizenbier* (wheat beer), found in both *helles* (pale) and *dunkles* (dark) varieties, is growing in popularity. Very refreshing and slightly sweet tasting, wheat beer is unfiltered and thus naturally cloudy. Glass sizes vary, but common sizes are *kleines* (small, 300ml) and *grosses* (large, half litre). Weizenbier is traditionally served in half litre vase shaped glasses. *Radler* (shandy) is a 50/50 mix of beer and carbonated lemonade.

In Austria, as in Germany, beer and wine are both produced in large quantities. The Danube flows through two of Austria's principal wine-producing regions of Wachau (Stage 20), which produces high-quality white wines using Reisling grapes and the Viennese Weinviertel wine quarter (Stage 22). Here villages such as Grinzing and Nussdorf are famous for the production of *heurige* wines, young fruity white wine produced mainly from Grüner Veltliner grapes and often served directly from the barrel.

Hungary and Slovakia have long histories of wine production with vineyards spread throughout Hungary and neighbouring parts of southern Slovakia. Quality suffered from a pursuit of quantity during the communist era, but has been steadily recovering since. In Hungary, large quantities of table wine are produced from Kadarka red grapes or Olasz white grapes (a variety of Riesling). Better known are full-bodied golden white wines, slightly sweet but fiery and peppery and an ideal accompaniment to spicy Hungarian food, and Bull's Blood, a full-bodied red made from Bikavér grapes. Most famous of all is Tokay, a dessert wine from north-east Hungary made by a unique process where the sweet pulp of over-ripe rotted Furmint grapes (known as Aszú) is added to barrels of one-year-old wine and left to mature for at least three more years. Unicum is a herbal liquer; while *Pálinka* fruit brandy, usually made from plums or apricots, is the national spirit.

All the usual soft drinks (colas, lemonade, fruit juices, mineral waters) are widely available. Apple juice mixed 50/50 with carbonated water and known as *apfelschorle* is widely consumed in Germany and Austria. *Most* and *birne-most* are rough cider-like alcoholic drinks in southern Germany and Austria produced from apples (most) or pears (birne-most). Tap water is safe to drink everywhere.

AMENITIES AND SERVICES

Grocery shops
All cities, towns and larger villages passed through have grocery stores, often supermarkets, and most have

The Mugln fountain in Tulln was constructed from stones dredged from the Danube (Stage 21)

pharmacies. Opening hours vary, but grocers in Germany close at 1300 on Saturdays and stay closed all day Sunday.

Cycle shops

The route is well provided with cycle shops, most with repair facilities. Locations are listed in the stage descriptions, but this is not exhaustive. Many cycle shops will adjust brakes and gears, or lubricate your chain, while you wait, often not seeking reimbursement for minor repairs. Touring cyclists should not abuse this generosity and always offer to pay, even if this is refused.

Currency and banks

Germany and Austria switched from national currencies to the Euro in 2002 and Slovakia joined the Eurozone in 2009. The Hungarian currency is the Forint, although many tourist oriented businesses such as hotels and restaurants will accept payment in Euros. Almost every town has a bank and most have ATM machines that enable transactions to be made in English. Travellers from the UK should contact their banks to confirm activation of bank cards for use in continental Europe.

Telephone and internet

The whole route has mobile phone (German *handy*) coverage. Contact your network provider to ensure your phone is enabled for foreign use with the optimum price package. To make an international call dial the international access code of the country you are in (00 or + in the UK), followed by the dialling code for the country you wish to reach:

- **+49** Germany
- **+43** Austria
- **+421** Slovakia
- **+36** Hungary
- **+44** UK

Most hotels, guest houses and hostels make internet access available to guests, often free but sometimes for a small fee.

Electricity
Voltage is 220v, 50Hz AC. Plugs are standard European two-pin round.

WHAT TO TAKE

Clothing and personal items
Despite the route being predominantly downhill, weight should be kept to a minimum. You will need clothes for cycling (shoes, socks, shorts or trousers, shirt, fleece, waterproofs) and clothes for evenings and days-off. The best maxim is two of each, 'one to wear, one to wash'. The time of year makes a difference as you need more and warmer clothing in April–May and September–October. All of this clothing should be capable of washing en route; a small tube or bottle of travel wash is useful. A sun hat and sunglasses are essential, while gloves and a woolly hat are advisable except in high summer.

In addition to your usual toiletries you will need sun cream and lip salve. You should take a simple first-aid kit. If staying in hostels you will need a towel and torch (your cycle light should suffice).

Cycle equipment
Everything you take needs to be carried on your cycle. If overnighting in accommodation, a pair of rear panniers should be sufficient to carry all your clothing and equipment, but if camping, you may also need front

Cumil the peeper bronze statue in Bratislava, said to be looking up ladies' skirts! (Stage 23)

41

panniers. Panniers should be 100 per cent watertight. If in doubt, pack everything inside a strong polythene lining bag. Rubble bags, obtainable from builders' merchants, are ideal for this purpose. A bar-bag is a useful way of carrying items you need to access quickly such as maps, sunglasses, camera, spare tubes, puncture-kit and tools. A transparent map case attached to the top of your bar-bag is an ideal way of displaying maps and guidebook.

Your cycle should be fitted with mudguards and bell, and be capable of carrying water bottles, pump and lights. Many cyclists fit an odometer to measure distances. A basic tool-kit should consist of puncture repair kit, spanners, Allen keys, adjustable spanner, screwdriver, spoke key and chain repair tool. The only essential spares are two spare tubes. On a long cycle ride, sometimes on dusty tracks, your chain will need regular lubrication and you should either carry a can of spray-lube or make regular visits to cycle shops. A good strong lock is advisable.

SAFETY AND EMERGENCIES

Weather
The upper Danube runs through the continental climate zone, typified by warm dry summers interspersed with short periods of heavy rain and cold winters. The beginning of Stage 1 is exposed to mountain weather with heavy winter snowfall, but this will have melted in most years by April.

Road safety
Throughout the route, cycling is on the right side of the road. If you have never cycled before on the right you will quickly adapt, but roundabouts may prove challenging. You are most prone to mistakes when setting off each morning. One-way streets often have signs permitting contra-flow cycling.

Much of the route is on dedicated cycle paths, but care is necessary as these are sometimes shared with pedestrians. Use your bell, politely, when approaching pedestrians from behind. Where you are required to cycle on the road there is usually a dedicated cycle lane.

Many city and town centres have pedestrian only zones. These restrictions are often only loosely enforced and you may find locals cycling within them, indeed many zones have signs allowing cycling.

None of the countries passed through require compulsory wearing of cycle helmets, but their use is recommended. Modern lightweight helmets with improved ventilation have made wearing them more comfortable.

Emergencies
In the unlikely event of an accident, the standardised EU emergency phone number is 112. The entire route has mobile phone coverage. Provided you have an EHIC card issued by

Passau cathedral organ is the largest in Europe (Stage 14)

your home country, medical costs of EU citizens are covered under reciprocal health insurance agreements, although you may have to pay for an ambulance and claim the cost back through insurance.

Theft
In general the route is safe and the risk of theft very low, particularly in Germany and Austria. However, you should always lock your cycle and watch your belongings, especially in cities. The risk of crime is higher in Slovakia and Hungary, although no great problem.

Insurance
Travel insurance policies usually cover you when cycle touring but they do not normally cover damage to, or

theft of, your bicycle. If you have a household contents policy, this may cover cycle theft, but limits may be less than the real cost of your cycle. Cycle Touring Club (CTC; www.ctc. org.uk) offers a policy tailored for your needs when cycle touring.

ABOUT THIS GUIDE

Text and maps
There are 29 stages, each covered by a separate map drawn to a scale of 1:150,000. At this scale it is not practical to cycle the route using only these maps, and local more detailed maps are advised. However, in Germany and Austria, signposting and waymarking are generally good; these combined with the stage

descriptions and maps in this guide should be sufficient to cycle much of the route without the expense or weight of carrying a large number of other maps. Beware, however, as the route described here does not always exactly follow the waymarked route.

Place names on the maps that are significant for route navigation are shown in **bold** in the text. The abbreviation 'sp' in the text indicates a signpost. Distances shown are cumulative within each stage. For each city, town and village passed an indication is given of facilities available (accommodation, refreshments, YH, camping, tourist office, cycle shop, station) when the guide was written. This list is neither exhaustive nor does it guarantee that establishments are still in business. No attempt has been made to list all such facilities as this would require another book the same size as this one. For fuller listings of accommodation, contact local tourist offices and/or search online. Tourist offices along the route are listed in Appendix E.

While route descriptions were accurate at the time of writing, things do change. Temporary diversions may be necessary to circumnavigate improvement works and permanent diversions to incorporate new sections of cycle track. The Danube is prone to occasional flooding, indeed exceptionally high floods in 2013 caused considerable damage, blockage to the route and diversions. In these instances you will usually find signs showing recommended diversions, although these may be in local languages only.

Some alternative routes exist. Where these offer a reasonable variant, usually because they are either shorter or offer a better surface, they are mentioned in the text and shown in blue on the maps.

Language

The English spelling of Danube is used throughout. In German the river is known as the Donau, in Slovak it is the Dunaj and in Hungarian the Duna. An exception is made for compound proper nouns (Donauquelle, Donauradweg and Mosoni Duna, for example). Place names and street names are given in appropriate local languages, apart from *Wien, Munchen* and *Bayern*, where the English-language names Vienna, Munich and Bavaria have been used. In the text the German ß (known as an eszett) is shown and pronounced as double ss. On the maps it appears as ß. See Appendix C for a list of useful German and Hungarian words.

STAGE 1

Martinskapelle to Donaueschingen

Start	Martinskapelle, Bregquelle (1094m)
Finish	Donaueschingen, Donauquelle (678m)
Distance	39.5km
Waymarking	Bregtalweg (from Furtwangen to Bräunlingen)

The first stage starts by descending through Schwarzwald, at first on a quiet country road and then along the course of a dismantled railway. The route follows the river Breg through the Bregtal Valley, passing a number of small towns, before emerging from the forest into an open agricultural area known as the Baar Plateau. The stage ends at Donaueschingen where the Breg and Brigach rivers combine to become the Danube. The common theme along this stage is a steady descent on good-quality gravel tracks with just two short climbs to cross low ridges.

Getting to the source

▶ Turn R outside **Triberg station** following station approach road with a massive steam railway engine R. Pass over road bridge, with railway R and turn immediately L, sharply downhill on an asphalt track. At bottom turn L again into Fréjus Strasse (B500, part of Schwarzwald Panoramaweg). Pass under bridge you have just come over and continue uphill on Hauptstrasse through the pretty, and much-visited, town of **Triberg** (accommodation, refreshments, YH, tourist office, cycle shop, station). Follow main road round sharp right-hand bend and fork L uphill (Clemens-Maria-Hofbauer-Strasse). Clemens-Maria-Hofbauer-Strasse is a short-cut, bypassing next hairpin bend on main road.

Pass Wallfahrtskirche church L and turn L 100m after church back onto main road. Pass small Bergsee lake L, then follow road as it winds uphill with **Triberg waterfalls**, the highest in Germany, in forest L. Continue

The shortest route (12km) to the Bregquelle Danube source requires cycling from Triberg station (617m) to Martinskappelle along quiet roads with two climbs and a total ascent of almost 500m.

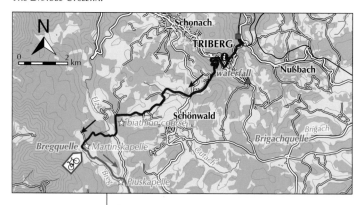

map continues
on page 48

ahead at roundabout through hamlet of Im Loch (accommodation, refreshments). Pass R turn to Schönach then turn R (Schwarzenbach) at next turn beside Die Inselklause Hotel. Follow gently undulating road as it winds past series of farms and becomes Weissenbach. Climb back into forest and bear L (Katzensteigstrasse), passing **biathlon course** in trees L. Drop downhill and

Martinskapelle sits above the Bregquelle on the watershed between the Rhine and Danube

after 800m leave road by turning R onto cycle track into trees (Elztalweg). Continue on winding good-quality gravel track ascending through forest, forking R, L (Brücklerainweg), L again and finally R at series of well marked forest path junctions following yellow and blue cycle track signs, passing en route a small spring L, source of River Elz (which flows north into the Rhine).

After 1.5km, at summit of track (1102m), emerge onto quiet road (Farnwaldstrasse). Turn L, passing Zur Martinskapelle refuge R (accommodation, refreshments) and L again past **Martinskapelle** chapel to reach Kolmenhof car park (12km, 1094m) L (accommodation, refreshments). ▶ From here, footpath leads 50m into meadow R to reach the Danube source.

Near the chapel you cross the main European watershed between the Rhine (flowing north-west to the North Sea) and the Danube (flowing south-east to the Black Sea).

Bregquelle, the true Danube source, is a rock-lined basin in meadows close to Kolmenhof. This is actually the source of the Breg, the longer of two tributaries that meet at Donaueschingen to form the Danube (the other, Brigach, rises 10km east of here). Two plaques beside the basin state that the river flows 2888km from the Black Forest to the Black Sea, with the first 647km through Germany.

The designation of Bregquelle as the true Danube source was the subject of legal dispute in 1965, when the council in nearby Furtwangen applied to have the Bregquelle officially recognised as the source. Objections by residents of Donaueschingen, where a small spring near to the confluence of the Breg and Brigach had officially been called the Donauquelle (Danube source) since Roman times resulted in a compromise, with the Bregquelle being termed the 'Danube headwater' and the spring in Donaueschingen retaining the title of 'official source'.

The main route begins from the Breg source at **Martinskapelle** and follows the quiet country road (Farnwaldstrasse) downhill past a series of farms with the infant Breg R. After 2km reach **Piuskapelle** R and turn R

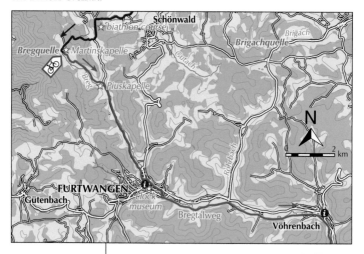

at T-junction (Katzensteigstrasse). Soon cross Breg for first time and continue downhill past more farms to reach beginning of **Furtwangen** (7km, 862m) (accommodation, refreshments, tourist office, cycle shop).

> **Furtwangen** (pop. 9250) is the first town on the Breg, and hence on the Danube. In the 19th century its main industry was clock making, which was particularly boosted by the high-quality musical clocks produced by the factory of Emilian Wehrle. These signalled the hour with a variety of different sounds including flutes, trumpets, birdsong and animal noises. Today the city's German clock and watch museum (*Deutsches Uhrenmuseum*) and its university, which has departments of microelectronics and precision engineering, reflect this history.

Turn R (Bismarckstrasse) and fourth L (Grieshaberstrasse). Cross Breg and bear R (Allmendstrasse). Pass bus station and high school R, then just before reaching Rewe supermarket turn R (Auf dem Moos), recrossing river. Cross main road and turn immediately L (Am

Niegenhirschwald). Follow this road into open country and when it ends, continue ahead on good-quality gravel cycle track (**Bregtalweg**) along course of Bregtalbahn railway (closed 1972), with Breg L. At beginning of Vöhrenbach, pass swimming baths L and follow Schwimmbadstrasse ahead into Bahnhofstrasse to reach bus station on site of old **Vöhrenbach** railway station (15km, 802m) (accommodation, refreshments, tourist office).

Continue along cycle track parallel with main road for 300m, then bear R into Auf der Wehrte. Where this ends, continue ahead along cycle track with forest R and river L. After 3km, cross a road leading R into Linachtal valley.

Linachtal is the location of the **Linachtalsperre**, an early hydro-electric station and reinforced concrete dam with unusual arched lattice work construction that, having closed in 1969, was restored and reactivated in 2007 to provide power for the local community. The Stausee lake, above the dam, is being developed as a tourist attraction.

Soon after Linachtal, pass small bridge L leading across river to *gasthaus* on main road (accommodation,

map continues on page 50

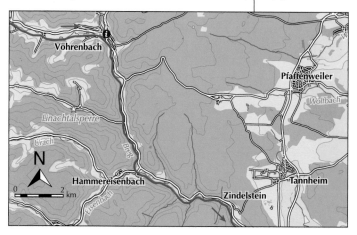

49

refreshments). Continue on cycle track and cross main road that leads to **Hammereisenbach** R (20.5km, 755m) (accommodation, refreshments).

Continue ahead onto road passing old station and new houses and where this ends follow cycle track ahead between forest R and river L. Passing small farm after 2km, dogleg R and L across sidestream. After another 2km pass road leading L across river to hamlet of **Zindelstein** (refreshments) and dogleg R and L.

Shortly before **Wolterdingen** (28km, 718m) (refreshments), cycle track bears R into forest, temporarily diverging from railway course to avoid a flood protection dam built across old route. Climb over low forested ridge, then drop down and bear L just before reaching a road. Continue through trees, passing timber yard L, to emerge onto side road at point where it reaches main road. Turn L onto main road and immediately R into farm lane (sp Bräunlingen) following this for 800m to regain course of old railway. Recross main road and continue past hamlet of Bruggen. When reaching main road again, turn R on cycle track beside road, which leads into beginning

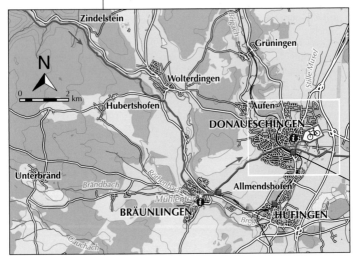

of Bräunlingen. Turn R at T-junction and follow road (Bruggener Strasse) as it bears L into centre of **Bräunlingen** R (34.5km, 693m) (accommodation, refreshments, camping, tourist office, cycle shop, station).

> Despite being surrounded by German states, **Bräunlingen** (pop. 4125) was Austrian territory until 1806, when Napoleon's redrawing of the map of Europe incorporated the town within the Grand Duchy of Baden. As an Austrian enclave it missed the German Protestant Reformation and remained strongly Catholic. Although fires destroyed many of the town's older buildings over the years, and others were ruined during the Second World War, the Mühlentor old city gate and parish church of St Remigius remain.

Continue through **Mühlentor** city gate into Hüfinger Strasse. Cross Breg and after 200m turn L into Donaueschinger Strasse. Immediately after station R, cycle track commences L of road. Follow this for 3km, climbing over a small ridge, to reach outskirts of Donaueschingen.

Bear R and follow Bräunlinger Strasse, descending steeply into Brigachtal valley. At bottom of hill continue over railway bridge into Bahnhofstrasse to reach **Donaueschingen** station R (accommodation, refreshments, tourist office, cycle shop, station). At roundabout in front of station, turn L (Josefstrasse) and follow this over river Brigach. After bridge, bear R (An der Stadtkirche) to reach St Johann church R. Behind this church, down a flight of steps, is the **Donauquelle**, 'official' source of the Danube (39.5km, 678m).

> **Donaueschingen** (pop. 21,300) sits astride the Brigach, 1.5km above its confluence with the Breg. The town became the seat of the Fürstenberg family in the 13th century, and the present Schloss Fürstenberg palace was built in 1723 before being remodelled in neo-baroque style during 1893–1896; the family still live here. A large landscaped

park can be found next to the palace. In a corner of this park – between the palace and St Johann parish church – is the Donauquelle, where a white marble monument and reflecting pool marks the 'official' source of the Danube. The monument originally stood outside the town on Schützenberg hill. It consists of a group of figures with 'mother Baar' showing the way of the river to her daughter 'young Danube'. A small stream (the official Danube) runs from the monument to join the Brigach after 100m.

The Fürstenberg family have long been patrons of the arts, and a major contemporary music festival is held in the town every autumn. In the centre of town a quirky bronze fountain featuring a group of musicians reflects this association and in his novel, *Dr Faustus*, Thomas Mann credited Donaueschingen as a centre of new music.

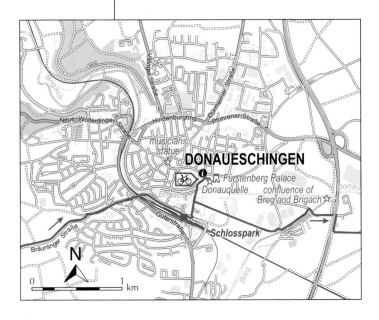

Musicians fountain in Donaueschingen

STAGE 2
Donaueschingen to Tuttlingen

Start	Donaueschingen, Donauquelle (678m)
Finish	Tuttlingen, Rathausbrücke bridge (645m)
Distance	35.5km
Waymarking	Donau Radweg, Deutsche Donau

The route continues across the Baar plateau as far as Geisingen, and then enters the beginning of the limestone Donautal gorge through the hills of the Schwäbische Alb. This is typical karst country – the Donauversickerung, an area of seasonal sinkholes, where the Danube disappears underground during dry weather, lies between Immendingen and Möhringen. The stage ends at the light industrial town of Tuttlingen.

To visit the confluence of Breg and Brigach (another 'official' Danube source), do not cross river but continue ahead on track parallel to Breg for 250m.

Pfohren is known for its storks, with three nests and a stork statue in the village centre.

Storks' nest statue in Pfhoren

From the **Donauquelle** in Donaueschingen, retrace your route along An der Stadtkirche into Josefstrasse. Cross **Brigach** and after 150m turn L (Prinz-Fritzi-Allee). At end continue ahead on cycle track through **Schlosspark**. Pass athletics stadium L and bear R (still Prinz-Fritzl-Allee) parallel to Breg R. At end turn R (Brigachweg), crossing the **Breg**. ◀ Continue under road bridge, then turn R by entrance to sewerage works and L after 200m into open country.

Follow asphalt track for 2km winding R and L through fields. Turn R at crossing of tracks and bear L at T-junction. At main road, turn L over Danube (your first crossing of the 'official' Danube), passing church L, and follow Hüfinger Strasse into **Pfohren** (5.5km, 675m) (refreshments, camping). ◀

Pass stork statue R and turn immediately R (Wiesenstrasse), passing 15th-century **Entenburg hunting lodge** R, which looks like a large barn conversion. When this street bears L, continue ahead (Birchring). After last house R, turn R on cycle track behind houses.

Follow track through fields and along riverbank. Pass under road bridge and bear immediately L parallel to main road. After 500m, turn R through fields with river meandering R. Pass bridge R (which leads to Neudingen (accommodation, refreshments)) and after 200m turn L beside barn, continuing to wind through fields for 2.5km. Turn L at T-junction, then R alongside main road. Take second turn L under the road and turn R along other side of road. Follow cycle track, eventually bearing away from road, circling below the old volcanic cone of **Wartenberg hill** (845m), which rises L. Dogleg L and R across a road coming down from hill and continue to reach a road. Turn R, and after 100m R again (Hauptstrasse). Continue ahead over roundabout into **Geisingen** (15.5km, 667m) (accommodation, refreshments, cycle shop, station).

Situated on the eastern edge of the Baar plateau, **Geisingen** (pop. 6000) was an important medieval town. A long period of decline set in after capture in 1632 by Swedish forces during the Thirty Years'

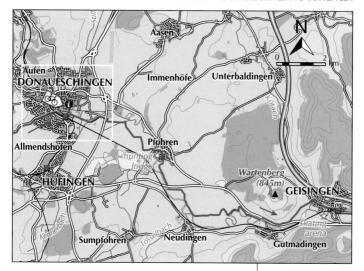

map continues
on page 56

War, with the town eventually losing its charter. A post-Second World War revival led to a new charter in 1956. The most notable building is an indoor in-line skating arena, the first in Germany, which has 3000 seats and an outdoor 480m track built to world championship standards.

Turn R at end of Hauptstrasse (Engenerstrasse). Cross railway level crossing and turn L (Riedweg) on track parallel to railway. Continue for 2.5km, passing under motorway and road bridges. Shortly after a weir R, bear R away from main railway and pass under another railway. Bear L beside this line, then R onto bridge across Danube. Cross main road and turn L onto cycle track beside road. Turn R (Ortsstrasse) and bear R (still Ortsstrasse) into **Hintschingen** (20km, 664m).

Turn L through village and where road bears sharply R, continue ahead between houses onto track through fields and alongside river. Turn L across river on **covered wooden bridge**, then follow road bearing R. Turn R (do not cross railway bridge) and pass **Zimmern station** L (accommodation, refreshments, station). Dogleg R and L to pass around railway depot and continue parallel with railway (Güterbahnhofstrasse) to reach back of **Immendingen station**. Pass under station footbridge, and turn sharply R up ramp onto this bridge and across railway. Descend ramp, turning R (Bahnhofstrasse) and immediately R on cycle track behind shops (Blumenweg). Continue into Blumenstrasse, passing an ornately decorated house, then turn L (Brunnenstrasse) to reach centre of **Immendingen** (23.5km, 667m) (accommodation, refreshments, station).

Track ahead leads to Donauversickerung (camping, refreshments) although a better view of the dry riverbed can be found 1.5km further along the main route.

Follow Brunnenstrasse, bearing R past Gasthof Kreuz, and turn R (Donaustrasse). Cross railway level crossing and continue ahead on cycle track, crossing Danube by another covered wooden bridge with weir R. Continue into Unterer Ösch, parallel to railway, passing under road bridge. Pass sewerage works R to reach crossing of tracks. ◄

Between Immeldingen and Möhringen lies the **Donauversickerung**, a limestone area of sinkholes

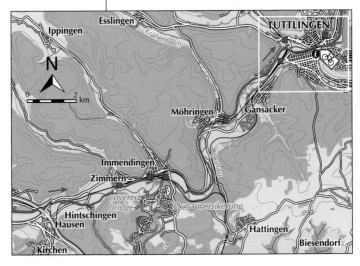

56

and underground river systems where – during periods of dry weather – the Danube disappears underground and leaves a dry riverbed, which can be walked on. The water flows south for 14km before reappearing at Aachquelle and flowing as the Aach into Bodensee. This is a legacy of past geological events, when the Rhine captured the upper waters of the Danube, and an underground network of streams connects the two basins.

The number of days when Danube water flows into the Rhine has been steadily increasing over the centuries and the total has now reached over 270 per year. It is expected that at some time in the future, seasonal flows will become permanent and all water in this stretch of the Danube will flow south into Bodensee and the Rhine.

It is possible to cycle across the dry riverbed downstream of the sinkholes near Immendingen

Turn L over river and bear R winding through fields between railway L and river R. Pass a turning R, which in dry conditions leads across the Danube riverbed to villages on the other bank. Continue for 4km, crossing under road bridge and continue following railway past tennis club R into **Möhringen**. Continue into Im Anger and turn L over railway level crossing beside Möhringen Rathaus railway station (29km, 658m) (accommodation, refreshments, station).

Turn immediately R after crossing railway (Hermann-Leiber-Strasse and R at T-junction (Marktgasse). Follow this street bearing L, cross a small stream and turn L at next T-junction (Am Schaftmarkt). Continue ahead over crossroads into Gihrsteinstrasse and turn R (Anton Braun Strasse) then L (Bleicherstrasse). Turn sharply R at end (Am Mühlberg) and leave Möhringen on cycle track with wooded hillside rising L and water meadows R. After 2.5km, emerge onto Oberer Bann. ◄

Continue ahead with river R and where road bears L away from river continue ahead on cycle track along riverbank. Dogleg L and R over sidestream, then turn R to return to riverbank. Pass under three railway bridges and a road bridge in quick succession and continue through parkland. Pass under two pedestrian bridges to

Turning on R leads over Danube to a steam and model railway museum (very limited opening hours), with some old steam locomotives visible in railway sidings R.

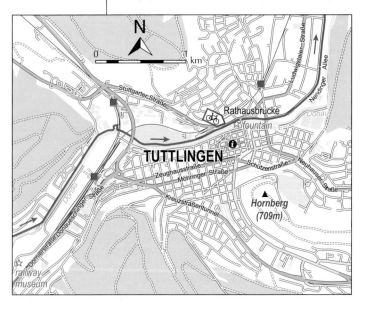

The water jet and the modern covered Rathausbrücke bridge in Tuttlingen

reach main road at point where **Rathausbrücke covered pedestrian bridge** leads R across Danube into centre of **Tuttlingen** (35.5km, 645m) (accommodation, refreshments, camping, tourist office, cycle shop, station).

Tuttlingen (pop. 27,000) town centre is built on a grid pattern with wide streets and classically designed buildings, the result of rebuilding after a fire that completely destroyed the city in 1803. Rising above Tuttlingen, the wooded Hornberg hill (709m) is topped by the ruins of a 15th-century castle. Destroyed in 1645 during the Thirty Years' War, the remains were used as a source of stone for the 1803 reconstructions.

In 1867 Gottfried Jetter began production of medical equipment here, thus setting the scene for the town to become a major producer of surgical instruments and medical appliances. Nowadays a cluster of over 300 companies produce 50 per cent of worldwide output of such products. Streets and roundabouts are named after major manufacturers and an exhibition of historical and modern surgical appliances can be found at ACIG. It is a sobering thought that if you have an operation in hospital, many of the instruments used will have been made in Tuttlingen.

STAGE 3
Tuttlingen to Sigmaringen

Start	Tuttlingen, Rathausbrücke bridge (645m)
Finish	Sigmaringen bridge (571m)
Distance	54.5km
Waymarking	Deutsche Donau, D6 and EV6

The backdrop to this stage is one of stunning karst scenery, with the route following the Danube as it cuts the narrow twisting Donautal gorge through the forested limestone hills of the Swäbische Alb. No major towns are passed, but there is a string of small villages along the floor of the gorge and castles perched on the cliffs above. The whole area is part of the Obere Donau Nature Park, which is home to a number of rare mammals including lynx and chamois inhabiting the hills and beaver in the rivers.

From N end of **Rathausbrücke bridge** in Tuttlingen, follow cycle track E beside Untere Vorstadt with Danube and **Donaufontaine fountain** R. Bear R passing under Gross Brück bridge and continue along riverbank into Dammstasse. At next bridge, continue ahead (**Nendinger Allee**) with cycle track R. Pass industrial estate L and at roundabout keep ahead under first exit road. Cross railway level crossing, then turn R and bear R to follow cycle track beside railway for 2km to reach **Nendingen** (5km, 637m) (accommodation, refreshments, station).

Turn R over level crossing, then R (Industriestrasse) and L at end (Sattlerstrasse). Keep ahead over crossroads (Austrasse) to leave village on cycle track between fields. After 2km reach **Stetten** (refreshments, station), entering village on Bachstrasse. Continue into Josef-Lang-Strasse, cross railway bridge and turn R parallel to railway (Eisenbahnstrasse) with view of **Mühlheim Oberstadt** across valley R. Drop downhill at end of village and bear R on cycle track beside railway, then continue ahead

(Griesweg) into **Mühlheim** (9km, 638m) (accommodation, refreshments, station).

Turn L onto main road (no cycle lane) and after passing factories R, turn R and immediately L onto quiet country road. Pass chapel and cemetery R, then at T-junction where wooded hillside rises ahead, turn R onto cycle track. This drops downhill past **Mülheim Nature Reserve** for beavers then winds for 4km through a narrow gorge, with railway and river R. Emerge onto road and pass timber yard L. Bear R at beginning of **Fridingen** (accommodation, refreshments, cycle shop, station) and turn R on Oberer Damm to reach Fridingen bridge (15.5km, 624m).

Continue over main road (do not cross river) into Unterer Damm, with Danube R. At end of town, continue ahead on cycle track beside river. Bear L before sewerage works and continue past cliffside L. (Where the cycle track reaches the river, there is another series of sinkholes with water flowing underground to join the Rhine.) Turn R over river bridge and L to reach Ziegelhütte (refreshments). Danube now enters even narrower gorge bounded

Woodcarving of a beaver at entrance to Mülheim Nature Reserve

map continues on page 63

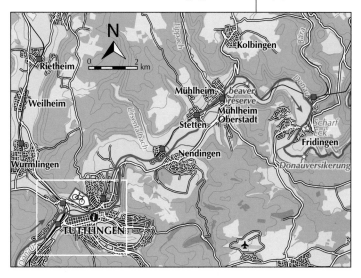

by steep limestone cliffs riddled with caves. Cycle track climbs over low wooded ridge (bypassing a tight river bend) then follows the side of the gorge past Bronner weir to reach **Jägerhaus** (accommodation, refreshments, camping) in a spectacular position surrounded by towering limestone pinnacles. Cycle track continues winding through gorge with Danube L. After 2.5km, shortly before railway bridge over river, turn R and L then climb to emerge on a country road just before **Beuron** (25km, 631m) (accommodation, refreshments, station). ◀

To visit Beuron, turn L on Abteistrasse over railway bridge.

Beuron is the site of a major Benedictine abbey. Originally founded as an Augustinian abbey in 1077, it was destroyed during the Thirty Years' War, then rebuilt, before being supressed in 1802 during the Napoleonic Wars. The Benedictines took over in 1863 and today 60 monks live and work here. With over 400,000 books, the abbey holds the largest monastic library in Germany. At the turn of the 20th century, the Beuron school was an art movement influenced by early Christian and Byzantine art. The largest collection of works from this movement can be found at Conception Abbey in Missouri, US.

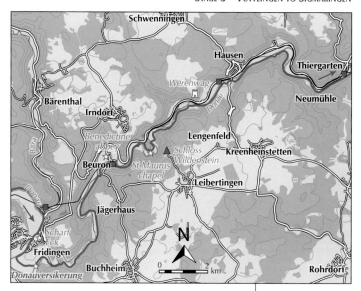

Dogleg L and R over road into Hubertusweg (do not cross railway) and continue on cycle track through gorge with railway and river L. After 2km, bear L under railway and turn R onto suspension bridge over Danube. Turn R along riverbank, then climb up over railway tunnel mouth and bear R onto quiet road. Pass **St Maurus chapel** and continue ahead through meadows, then fork R to cross river at next bridge. Turn L past Donauhaus and continue on cycle track as it follows the river with steep wooded slopes R. Pass Talhof (on opposite bank of river), climb through forest then fork L downhill back to river meadows. Turn R before bridge (do not cross river), passing below **Schloss Werenwag** castle perched on clifftop L. Continue through gorge between cliffs R and Danube L to reach road by bridge to **Hausen** (33km, 598m) (accommodation, refreshments, camping, cycle shop, station). ▶

Dogleg L and R across road, then follow cycle track as it winds in and out of forest through the gorge, to reach

map continues on page 64

To visit Hausen, cross river and turn R. Return the same way.

Schloss Werenwag stands high above the Donautal gorge

Neumühle (accommodation, refreshments) after 4.5km. Continue along gorge, crossing railway level crossing, to reach road by bridge leading to **Thiergarten** (accommodation, refreshments, station).

Turn R following road (do not cross bridge) and where this ends at **Käppeler Hof** (refreshments) continue ahead on cycle track past St Georges chapel R. Cross Danube by next bridge, then bear R on cycle track beside

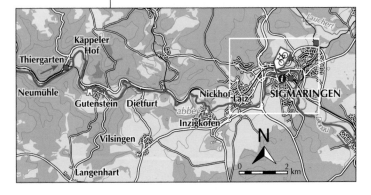

main road. Follow this as it bears R away from road under railway bridge. Emerge onto quiet road and turn R at crossroads (Burgfeldenstrasse) passing Schloss Gutenstein castle R. Continue over river bridge into **Gutenstein** (43.5km, 591m) (accommodation, refreshments).

Continue through village (still Burgfeldenstrasse) and turn L (Hohenbergstrasse) into easily missed turn just after St Gallus parish church. Cross railway level crossing and turn R onto cycle track parallel to railway. Follow track bearing L then climbing steeply for short distance before dropping down R round next bend in river. Cross Danube by suspension bridge and continue along riverbank. Pass under railway bridge and continue on cycle track to reach road by bridge leading to **Dietfurt** (accommodation, refreshments).

Continue across road (do not cross river) and follow cycle track beside railway line. After 1km, cycle track briefly passes L under railway then R across a side stream, before returning to run between river and railway through narrow part of gorge. Follow track circling a wooded hillside, then return to railway and continue to road by old (closed) Inzighofen station. Turn R, over Danube bridge and follow road round hairpin bend climbing steeply out of gorge past **Nickhof** (accommodation). Just before second bend after Nickhof, bear L on cycle track into woods. Continue through abbey garden and descend under archway into the *kloster* (abbey) at **Inzigkofen** (50.5km, 615m) (accommodation, refreshments). Continue ahead out of abbey and turn L by car park onto cycle track that leads through fields to Laiz.

Pass football pitch R and continue ahead (Inzighofer Strasse) to reach riverbank. Cross main road in **Laiz** (accommodation, refreshments) into Uferweg and continue on cycle track passing Laiz wier L. Cycle under road bridge, then pass swimming pool R. Bear L past campsite R. Pass under road bridge and pass footbridge. Where stage ends at second road bridge, with Schloss Sigmaringen castle rising ahead, you can turn R (Burgstrasse) to reach centre of **Sigmaringen** (54.5km, 571m) (accommodation, refreshments, YH, camping,

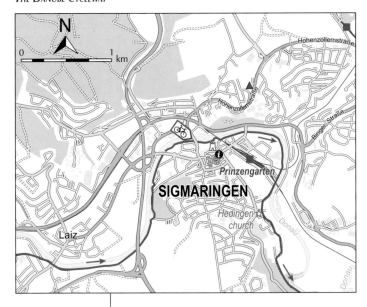

tourist office, cycle shop, station) or continue ahead beside river onto next stage.

Sigmaringen (pop. 16,500) is dominated by the huge Schloss Sigmaringen, the ancestral home (since 1535) to the Hohenzollern-Sigmaringen – the junior branch of a family whose senior branch (the Hohenzollerns) provided the kings of Prussia and the kaisers of Imperial Germany. In 1866, Prince Charles of Sigmaringen was invited to become the first king of Romania, taking the title of Prince Carol. His brother Leopold was offered the Spanish throne in 1870, but he backed out when French objections triggered the Franco-Prussian War. The castle, with sumptuous residential apartments, precious artworks and one of the world's largest private collections of ancient weapons, can be visited on guided tours.

Other important sights include Leopoldplatz and Karlstrasse, where there are many notable buildings and the English-style Prinzengarten. Hedingen church contains the graves of the Sigmaringen princes.

STAGE 4
Sigmaringen to Riedlingen

Start	Sigmaringen bridge (571m)
Finish	Riedlingen bridge (528m)
Distance	33.5km
Waymarking	Deutsche Donau, D6, EV6

After a short final section of gorge, the Danube enters a wide agricultural valley. Always south of the river, with only a few short stretches along the riverbank, the route follows a mix of quiet country roads and surfaced field paths. Beyond Mengen the going is level.

From underneath **Burgstrasse bridge** in Sigmaringen, take the cycle track E beside the Danube, passing below the imposing face of **Schloss Sigmaringen**. Turn L under railway bridge then follow cycle track beside river as it loops around town, dropping down L under a road bridge and then under two railway bridges. Emerge onto quiet road (Allee) and continue into Badstrasse, passing **Kloster Hedingen** church R. Pass sewerage works L and bear L onto cycle track leading into riverside woodland and follow this through fields for 2km to join Donaustrasse at beginning of **Sigmaringendorf** (5km, 567m) (accommodation, refreshments, station).

Bear R by Sigmaringendorf bridge, with Bruckkapelle bridge chapel R, and continue on riverside road (Krauchenweiser-Strasse). Where this turns away from

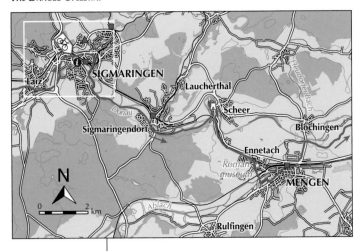

map continues
on page 70

river, bear L to follow cycle track through riverside wood-land. Where path forks, bear L to continue following river. At beginning of Scheer, bear L, passing under very low bridge (tall cyclists may need to duck) and continue past allotments to emerge on Mühlberg in **Scheer** (9km, 563m) (accommodation, refreshments).

> **Scheer** (pop. 2500) stands on a limestone bluff above a bend in the Danube where the river leaves the Donautal gorge and enters an alluvial plain. The main sights are the castle, built during 1485–1496 (it is a private residence that cannot be visited), the highly decorated St Nicholas parish church and the Loretto chapel.

Bear L (Fabrikstrasse), passing between **castle** R and old paper mill L. At end turn sharply R (Kirchberg), then after 50m, L and R into Hirsch-Strasse. Turn L (easy to miss, turn is opposite village pump) and R again into Donaustrasse along riverbank and continue past Scheer bridge. Where road turns away from river, continue ahead (Schaalstrasse). Turn R and continue across main

road into Bahnhofstrasse, then bear R over level crossing into Hipfelsberger Strasse, parallel to railway. Continue beside railway to reach Edelbrunnerweg in **Ennetach** (accommodation, refreshments). At end turn R (Scheerer Strasse). Where road bends L by **Roman museum** (*Römermuseum*), continue ahead (Mühlstrasse) between houses passing pasta factory R. Continue over level crossing, then follow cycle track under main road. Turn R, L and second L (Mühlgässe), circling swimming pools and tennis club. Pass sports fields, bear R by allotments and turn L (Messkircher Strasse) into **Mengen** (14km, 561m) (accommodation, refreshments, cycle shop, station).

The Roman museum in Ennetach holds finds from Acherberg Roman settlement

The Romans chose Acherberg hill, near **Mengen** (pop. 10,000), as the spot on which to build a fort to defend their border along the Danube. This was abandoned after AD70 when the Romans pushed north beyond the river, but a Roman village remained here until it was conquered by Alemanni tribes around AD230. Finds from this period are displayed in the Römermuseum. From 1276 to 1806, Mengen was part of the Habsburg Austrian Vorland. Many old, half-timbered houses remain from this period.

Continue through town (Hauptstrasse) to reach station roundabout. Bear R (Riedlingen Strasse). Just before next roundabout, bear L on cycle track then fork R and follow cycle track beside main road under railway and road bridges, and across roundabout out of Mengen. After 1km, shortly before road crosses Danube, turn R across road onto side road that winds between fields for 2.5km. Just before this road crosses Danube, turn R parallel to river onto cycle track between riverside trees L and fields R to reach Mühleweg. Turn L into beginning of **Hundersingen** and continue to reach bridge over Danube. ◄

From here a road leads over bridge into Hundersingen (21.5km, 545m) (accommodation, refreshments).

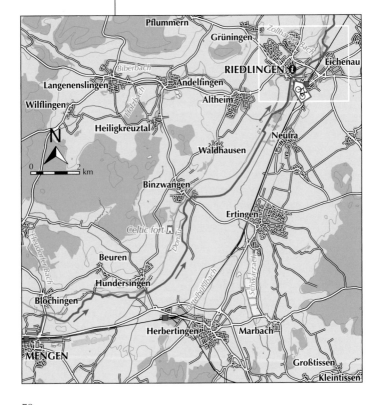

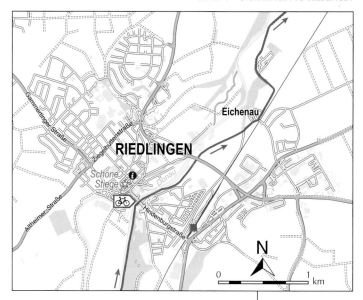

Turn R away from bridge and after 150m L onto cycle track through fields for 4.5km. On a buff above opposite side of Danube L, a large white construction is recreation of **Heuneberg Celtic fort** that once stood here. Just before Binzwangen, continue ahead beside sports field L then dogleg R and L across side road to reach main road that leads L into **Binzwangen** (26.5km, 538m) (accommodation, refreshments).

Go straight across main road onto Riedstrasse (do not turn L over Danube), passing between warehouses. After 150m turn R (Im Brühl), then fork L onto cycle track between fields. After 4km, at crossing of tracks turn L to reach Danube, then zig-zag L and R up onto flood dyke.

Cycle along flood dyke to reach **Riedlingen bridge** (33.5km, 528m) (accommodation, refreshments, camping, tourist office, station).

Riedlingen Marktplatz has many old buildings

Riedlingen (pop. 10,000) is a medieval town dating from 1247 that is centred around a historic market square. There are many half-timbered buildings dating from the 16th to the 18th centuries. The most notable, Schöne Stiege (1556), with an attractive outside wooden staircase, now houses the town museum.

STAGE 5
Riedlingen to Ehingen

Start	Riedlingen bridge (528m)
Finish	Ehingen station (509m)
Distance	37.5km
Waymarking	Deutsche Donau, D6, EV6

The Danube meanders through a wide valley with wooded hills never far away. The route, mostly on field paths, cuts across some of the meanders and as a result crosses the river nine times. This stage is mostly flat, but there are a few short climbs over low ridges.

From S end of **Riedlingen bridge**, follow Schlachthaus-strasse E beside Danube. Where this ends, continue beside river on cycle track and pass under road bridge. Emerge onto road and turn L to reach **Eichenau** (camping). Continue with railway line R (do not cross level crossing). Where road ends by sewerage works, pass through barrier and continue on cycle track through fields. Turn L alongside old water lily filled arm of Danube to reach a road and turn L over Danube towards **Daugendorf** (refreshments).

Turn immediately R through farmyard and continue to crossing of tracks. Turn R onto cycle track between fields. After 800m follow cycle track as it turns L and R. Pass first turn on L into **Bechingen** (refreshments), but after 175m turn L towards village. Before reaching village, turn R to reach road and follow this over Danube into **Zell** (accommodation, refreshments). Continue through village on Hauptstrasse. Cross railway bridge and turn L on cycle track beside railway. Cross Danube on joint railway/cycle bridge. When road is reached, turn L over level crossing and follow road into **Zwiefaltendorf** (9.5km, 526m) (accommodation, refreshments).

Zwiefaltendorf has a small castle (now an upmarket restaurant used mostly for weddings and corporate gatherings) and the Rössle, a small but renowned family run *brauerei* (brewhouse) producing beer, cider and schnapps. There is a stalactite-filled cave underneath the brewery, which was discovered in 1892 when excavations were being made to create a beer cellar. The cave fills with water from the Danube when the river is high.

Turn R in centre of village (Von-Speth-Strasse), pass castle R and cross Danube. Turn L through small car park onto cycle track beside railway. After 750m cross railway

map continues on page 76

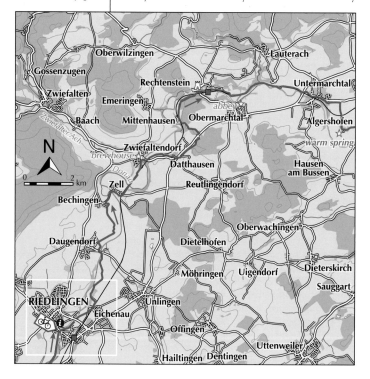

This rest place in Datthausen is a dedicated stop for cyclists

and pass trout farm and smokehouse L (refreshments), climbing steeply (20 per cent) for a short distance to hamlet of **Datthausen** (refreshments). At top, turn R by Radler-Rastplatz and then L into country road. ▶

Cross main road and turn L on cycle track beside road. Follow this as it swings away from road, then turns back passing under road. Turn R uphill to reach T-junction. Turn L and descend through fields and woods to join quiet road at **Mittenhausen**. Turn R (do not cross railway bridge) then continue on road through woods, over railway level crossing and turn L over Danube to reach **Rechtenstein** (16km, 525m) (accommodation, refreshments, station).

Turn R and immediately fork L uphill (Karl-Weiss-Srasse), then continue downhill (now Brühlhofstrasse). Continue through village, passing above **station** R. Immediately after railway level crossing turn L on cycle track parallel to railway, with onion-domed towers of **Kloster Obermarchtal abbey** visible across river R. After 2.5km, dogleg L and R across railway level crossing. Pass under modern road bridge and follow quiet road L (Ebene) then bear R (Bergstrasse) into **Untermarchtal** (21km, 517m) (accommodation, tourist office).

Radler-Rastplatz is a cycle rest place that, with a drinking water fountain and comfortable seating, allows you to recover from the climb.

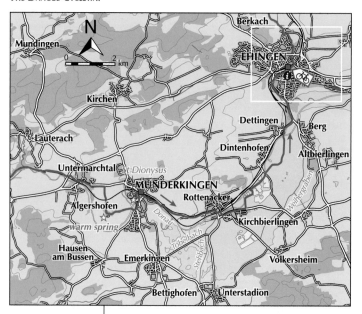

For Algershofen *warme quellen* (warm springs), turn R by old village pump, then R again for 500m. Bathing is possible in the murky water, which is at a constant temperature of 16°C. The springs are a breeding spot for European pond terrapins.

Turn L in village centre onto Munderkinger Strasse. As road leaves village, bear R onto cycle track beside road. After 800m, turn R on side road leading to **Algershofen**. ◄ Continue on road through village and cross Danube. Turn L (Hausener Strasse) and L again (Schillerstrasse). Turn L (Martinstrasse) and bear L to reach town hall (*rathaus*) in centre of **Munderkingen** (25km, 516m) (accommodation, refreshments, camping, station).

Munderkingen (pop. 5000), enclosed by a tight bend of the Danube, has a wealth of stepped gable and half-timbered medieval buildings including the town hall, Pfarrhof (former abbots residence) and Heilig-Geist-Spital (now the town museum). The parish church of St Dionysius is highly decorated with Gothic and Renaissance elements and a spectacular baroque altarpiece.

Turn R into Donaustrasse. Cross river and turn immediately R on cycle track through gardens, which bears L to emerge onto Bahnhofstrasse. Bear R and continue beside main road, crossing to L and back again, to reach **Rottenacker** (28.5km, 505m) (accommodation, refreshments, camping).

Just before road crosses Danube, turn L (Bahnhofstrasse) and R before hydro-electric power station on dual-use cycle/footbridge over weirs. Continue to reach main road (Kirchbierlinger Strasse) and turn L onto dual-use cycle/pedestrian path R of road. Cross

The ornate baroque altarpiece in St Dionysus church, Munderkingen

railway and switch to cycle track L of road before next side road. Turn L at end of built-up area between fields. Turn R after sewerage works and follow road winding between old gravel lakes and Danube for 1.5km. At road junction, where bridge L leads to **Dintenhofen**, fork R past sports fields L and continue on cycle track between fields. Continue across Danube and follow Höllweg into **Dettingen** (34km, 494m) (accommodation, refreshments). Cross railway level crossing and turn R (Rottenacker Strasse). Recross railway and follow cycle lane L of main road. Bear L at T-junction, still L of main road, passing factories.

Bear L at roundabout (Mühlweg) and after 1km turn R across road at traffic lights into narrow side road (Schwarze Gasse). Bear L (Mühlweg) and L again (Spitalstrasse) in front of **Liebfrauenkirche church**. Bear R (Untere Hauptstrasse) and turn L (Lederbruckgasse). Bear R (Tuchergasse) and continue into Am Viehmarkt. Pass

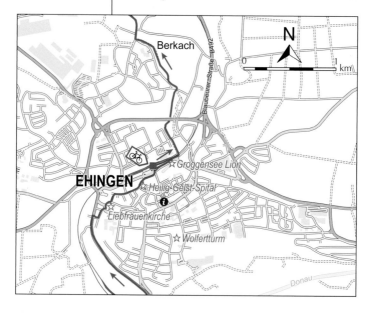

Heilig-Geist-Spital (local museum) and a preserved section of city wall, both R, then bear R (Hindenburgstrasse) to reach road junction opposite **Ehingen station** (37.5km, 509m) (accommodation, refreshments, tourist office, cycle shop, station).

This stone lion is part of the Groggensee war memorial in Ehingen

The medieval town of **Ehingen** (pop. 26,000) stands beside the Schmiech, a short distance above its confluence with the Danube. The town has a skyline marked by the spires of three significant churches: Liebfrauenkirche, St Blasius parish church and Konviktskirche. Other attractive buildings include the Heilig-Geist-Spital (1532), the Hohes Haus (pre-1400) and the half-timbered Spethsche hof (1624). Groggensee lake, watched over by an enormous stone lion, was created as a memorial to those who died in the First World War. The town calls itself the *Bierkulturstadt* (Beer Culture City), a claim based on the existence of four independent breweries that produce 43 different beers.

STAGE 6
Ehingen to Ulm

Start	Ehingen station (509m)
Finish	Ulm, Metzgerturm tower (471m)
Distance	41.5km
Waymarking	Deutsche Donau, Albdonaukreis 9

The route leaves the Danube on an attractive diversion up the Schmiech valley to Blaubueren for a visit to the spectacular Blautopf blue water lagoon, source of the Blau River. This river's valley is then followed to return to the Danube in the medieval cathedral city of Ulm. An alternative, more direct, route (signed D6, EV6) connects Ehringen and Ulm. This keeps closer to the Danube and is 8km shorter, but it is considerably less interesting.

From front of **Ehingen station**, cycle NW beside Pfisterstrasse between railway L and Groggensee R, passing First World War memorial (**stone lion**) R. Immediately after roundabout, turn L on cycle track under railway with River Schmiech R. Cross road into Schmiechtal and at end continue on cycle track. Pass under road bridge and continue through parkland. Cross road, turn L and immediately bear R on cycle track beside Rosenstrasse. Follow this passing behind houses and through fields. Turn R (Allmendinger Strasse) and follow this for 3.5km to reach **Allmendingen** (pop. 4500) (5.5km, 515m) (accommodation, refreshments, station).

Cycle ahead (Bergstrasse) and continue winding through village on Kleindorfer Strasse to reach **railway**. Immediately before level crossing, turn L on quiet road (Katzensteige) parallel to railway. After 2km dogleg R and L across a road onto cycle track through fields, and turn R alongside forest. Bear R onto Burrenweg, turn R (Brielgasse) and bend L (St Antoniusstrasse) into centre of **Schmiechen** (accommodation, refreshments, station).

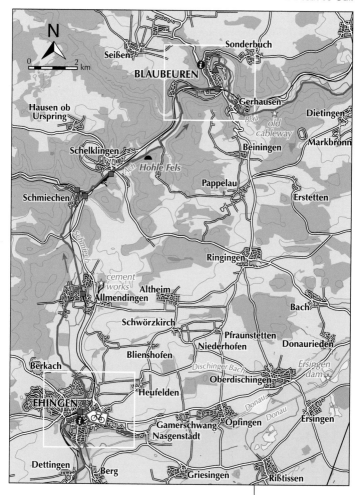

Turn R by parish church (Hauptstrasse) and bear L in front of station. Join cycle track L of road, cross level crossing and continue to reach **Schelklingen** (pop. 7000) (12km, 534m) (accommodation, refreshments, station).

map continues on page 84

81

Pass **Schelklingen station** R then cross main road at traffic lights and turn second R (Hohler-Felsen-Weg) under railway bridge. Bear L past limestone quarry and continue on cycle track, with wooded hillside rising R, passing **Hohle Fels cave** R.

Hohle Fels cave is an important Paleolithic archaeological site. A 15m passage leads to a 500m² cave, one of the largest in Germany. In the 19th century the cave was used as a source of bat guano for fertilizer and, during this time, animal bones of bear, mammoth, reindeer and wild horse were discovered. More recently, further excavations have uncovered evidence of human occupation during the Stone Age. Particularly significant among these are figurines carved from mammoth ivory and a 22cm-long nearly complete bone flute from 35,000BC. Believed to be the oldest human artworks discovered in the world, they can be seen in the Blaubeuren museum.

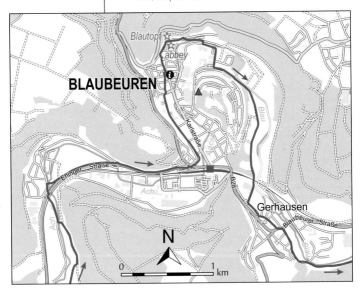

At end, turn L and after 275m turn R between fields.

At end, bear L across stream and turn R, cross level crossing and dogleg R and L across main road onto short cycle track to reach Aachtalstrasse. After 75m turn R (Wiesenweg) and continue on cycle track beside main road. At end, follow cycle track zigzagging R and L across two main roads into Weilerstrasse. At T-junction, dogleg R and L into Webergasse (cobbles) to reach town hall and Marktplatz in centre of **Blaubeuren** (20km, 522m) (accommodation, refreshments, YH, tourist office, cycle shop, station).

Blautopf lagoon in Blaubeuren has naturally occurring blue water

Blaubeuren (pop. 12,000) grew as a medieval town around an important Benedictine abbey (founded 1085, dissolved 1534 and used subsequently as a school) and a number of half-timbered buildings survive from this period. The abbey stands beside the Blautopf, a 21m-deep lagoon fed by water from a karst spring that runs blue due to natural chemical impurities in the water. It is one of Germany's largest springs and the source of the Blau River.

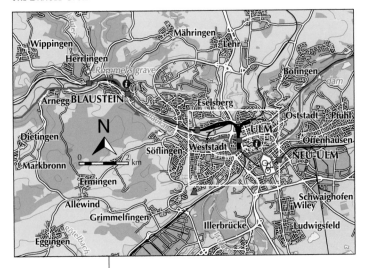

From the mid-19th century, local limestone from large quarries at Gerhausen was used to make cement, and a number of cement works grew-up. These grew in size and, under cartelisation in 1938, became part of Heidelberg Cement (Germany's largest cement producer), but most of them are now closed.

Continue ahead (Klosterstrasse) and turn R (Blautopfstrasse) to reach the **Blautopf blue water lagoon**. Bear R (Mühlweg) following Blau River downstream. Turn R across river on footbridge and immediately L (Dodelweg) circling sports club. At end turn L on cycle way along Blau River valley. Emerge onto Riedweg, pass under railway and turn L (Brunnenweg) and L again (Schulstrasse) passing through schoolyard into **Gerhausen** (23km, 508m) (refreshments, station).

Turn L (Blaubeurer Strasse) and R (Markbronner Strasse) and, just before bridge over Blau, fork R beside river. Fork R again before sewerage works and continue gently uphill along edge of woods, with hillside rising R, passing remains of **cableway**. ▶ Continue for 5km, with Blau meandering below L to reach beginning of **Arnegg** (refreshments).

Turn L and R into Oberer Wiesenweg, continuing past sports club L. At end turn L (Hauptstrasse) and continue into Kingensteiner Strasse. Just before end of village fork L on cycle track through fields and continue alongside Blau. Pass Herrlingen station on opposite side of river and turn L across river to edge of **Herrlingen** (pop. 3200) (32km, 496m) (accommodation, refreshments, station).

Turn R on cycle track beside railway. At end, dog-leg R and L into Ehrensteiner Strasse to reach centre of **Blaustein** (32.5km, 496m) (accommodation, refreshments, tourist office, cycle shop, station).

The cableway carried limestone across the valley from quarries to cement works before it was replaced by underground conveyors, which can be heard rattling in the background.

ERWIN ROMMEL

In the graveyard of St Andreas church, Herrlingen, is the burial place of Erwin Rommel (1891–1944), one of the most famous German military commanders during the Second World War. Rommel rose through the ranks in the First World War, fighting on the Italian Front, where he gained his first Iron Cross. Between the wars he taught at military academies, where his tactical strengths came to the notice of Adolf Hitler. His first field command was a Panzer tank division during the invasion of France (1940). However, it was as commander of the German Afrika Corps (1941–1943) that he became well known, during which time the allies nicknamed him 'the Desert Fox'. Rommel was regarded by friend and foe alike as a fair commander, who was considerate to POWs and who was reluctant to allow his troops to become involved in anti-semitic activities. After the allied invasion of Normandy (June 1944), where he commanded German defensive forces, Rommel became disillusioned with Hitler and became involved in the failed coup of 20 July 1944. Hitler, not wishing the bad propaganda that knowledge of Rommel's involvement would spark, offered him the chance to commit suicide, which he accepted by taking cyanide in Herrlingen on 14 October. It was claimed he died of injuries received in Normandy and he was buried with full military honours. The true version of events did not appear until after the war. The nearby Lindenhof, in part of which Rommel lived and which now houses a small Rommel museum, was originally a Jewish school – the teachers and pupils fled to Britain in 1933 after the rise of Nazism in Germany put their lives in danger.

Continue past Blaustein station R and shopping centre L. Just before railway bridge, dogleg L and R across main road onto cycle track that runs parallel to railway for 2km with allotments L. Pass under road bridge and bear R to follow Blau under railway. Emerge on cycle track beside Blaubeurer Strasse. Turn L, cross Blau and drop down L to pass under main road in **Söflingen** (37km, 483m) (accommodation, refreshments, cycle shop, station).

Turn R onto busy cycle route that passes through Ulm. Pass under Blaubeurer Strasse and continue beside Blau R past back of **Blautal shopping mall** L. Pass under road bridge and turn R on cycle track parallel to road. Continue past section of old city wall R and after 750m, at major road junction, turn L beside Neue Strasse. ◀ Pass under railway bridge and turn immediately L (do not continue under road bridge). Circle anti-clockwise on marked cycle track through bus station to climb up onto bridge beside railway. Continue beside railway and pass

Route through Ulm is subject to major roadworks lasting several years. Look out for signs showing diversionary routes.

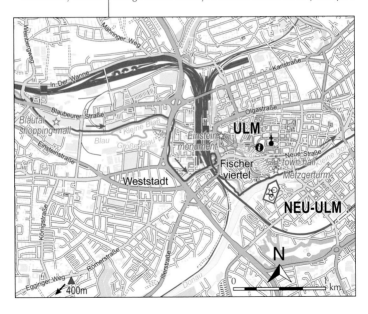

The spire of Ulm cathedral is the world's tallest church spire

under next road bridge. Bear L following asphalt track between allotments R and parkland L to reach banks of Danube. Turn L alongside river, with old city walls L, to reach gardens between **Metzgerturm** (Butchers' Tower) and **Ulm** (41.5km, 471m) (accommodation, refreshments, YH, tourist office, cycle shop, station).

ULM

The metropolitan area of Ulm (pop. 170,000, including Neu-Ulm) is made up of twin settlements, Ulm in Baden-Württemberg and Neu-Ulm across the Danube in Bavaria. Ulm developed as a free imperial city at the crossing of major east–west and north–south trading routes and had a flourishing early textile industry. In 1377, construction of a huge cathedral began, financed by local traders and guilds rather than Catholic authorities. Fuelled by a booming local economy, construction continued through the 15th and early 16th centuries. However, the Protestant Reformation and economic consequences of the Thirty Years' War caused construction to cease for over 200 years. Resuming in 1817, the cathedral was completed in 1890, financed by the proceeds of the Industrial Revolution. The spire was originally planned to be shorter but it was later increased to 161.5m so as to be four metres taller than Köln cathedral and become the tallest church spire in the world. Its 768 steps can be climbed, but the top section is open lattice work, which can seem quite airy – especially in windy conditions.

The city has lots of other historic buildings, many rebuilt after fire-bombing destroyed 80 per cent of the medieval city in December 1944. These include the medieval town hall and Krone inn (lodging place for the Holy Roman Emperor when visiting Ulm) as well as a number of medieval guild trading houses. The *Fischer Viertel* (fishermen's quarter) is a maze of cobbled streets with half-timbered houses. The most obvious modern building is the *stadtbibliothek* (city library), a glass pyramid beside the city hall. Albert Einstein (1879–1955) was born in a house on Bahnhofstrasse. A monument marks the spot, but the house was destroyed by WWII bombing. A very successful technical university (established in 1967) has seen Ulm become a magnet for high-tech activities, attracting research centres from major companies such as Daimler, Siemens and Nokia.

STAGE 7
Ulm to Lauingen

Start	Ulm, Metzgerturm tower (471m)
Finish	Lauingen Marktplatz (441m)
Distance	47.5km
Waymarking	Donau Radwanderweg, Deutsche Donau, D6, EV6

This stage, which is almost completely flat, involves crossing from Baden-Württemberg into Bavaria. Once clear of Ulm and its dormitory towns, the route passes through long stretches of riparian forest and skirts the Donaumoos, an area of low-lying fenland dotted with small lakes.

From riverside gardens in Ulm, between **Metzgerturm tower** and Danube, cycle NE on riverside cycle track beneath Ulm bridge and past section of old city walls

The route passes between Ulm city walls and Metzgerturm tower on one side and the Danube on the other

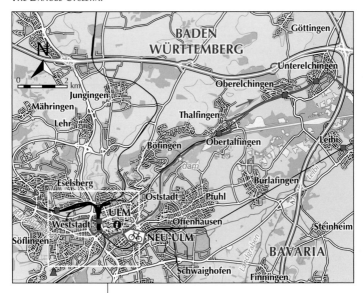

L. Pass under road bridge and bear R beside tram turning circle. Continue past **Böfingen dam** and hydroelectric power station R and through woodland, to enter Bavaria. Dogleg L and R across main road and continue on cycle track L of road. Immediately past St Thomas church, turn L (Donaustrasse) and continue over level crossing into **Thalfingen** (7km, 467m) (accommodation, refreshments, station).

Turn R at T-junction (Elchinger Strasse) and continue out of town, joining cycle track L. Pass through **Oberelchingen** (9.5km, 461m) (accommodation, refreshments, station) and continue to **Unterelchingen station** (11.5km, 458m) (accommodation, refreshments, station).

Immediately after station R, fork R (Lange Strasse) following railway for 500m. Turn R across level crossing and fork L (Weissinger Strasse). Continue on cycle lane R, going straight ahead at roundabout and over motorway bridge.

After 2.5km follow cycle lane bearing R away from road between fields, then bear R (Ortsstrasse) into hamlet

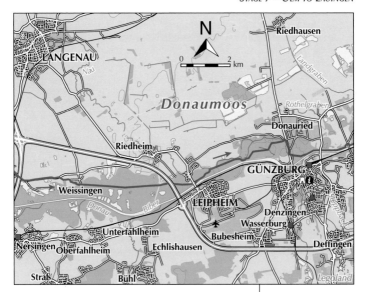

of **Weissingen** (15km, 458m) (refreshments). Bear R on gravel track into forest and continue under motorway to reach riverbank opposite **Leipheim** (20km, 452m) (accommodation, refreshments, camping (Riedheim), station).

map continues
on page 93

> The **Donaumoos**, a large area of 4000ha north of the Danube between Weissingen and Gundelfingen, was once part of the annual flood plain of the Danube, before hydrological improvements straightened and dammed the river behind flood dykes. It is an area of low-lying fenland and peaty soil, dotted by many small lakes. Three parts of the *moos* (fenland) are designated *Naturschutzgebiet* (nature protected areas). The moos is home to many rare animals, insects, birds and plants including *biber* (beaver), *brachvogel* (curlew) and orchids. It is a seasonal home to many breeding birds and an important stopover for migratory birds heading south across the Alps.

To visit Günzburg (accommodation, refreshments, YH, tourist office, cycle shop, station), continue ahead over Danube.

Do not cross river. Turn L under Leipheim bridge and after 150m turn briefly L away from river. Turn R onto Weidlenweg and follow this into woodland. Turn R on gravel track and continue for 3.5km winding through forest. Emerge onto quiet road and turn R to reach main road at **Donauried** (accommodation, refreshments). Turn R (Heidenheimer Strasse) on cycle track L. Pass car dealership R, cross Nau stream and turn L into forest. ◀

Günzburg (modern pop 20,000) was developed to control an important crossing point over the river, after the Romans had extended their empire across the Danube in AD75. A period of decline after the Romans left in the fifth century ended when the city came under the control of the Austrian Habsburgs, who held it for over 500 years (1301–1805). During this time it became an important centre within the Austrian Vorland, housing an imperial palace and a mint. After capture by Napoleon, Günzburg became a reluctant part of Bavaria (1806), a result of the treaty of Pressburg, and has remained German ever since.

The historical centre has many listed buildings from the Austrian era including the Frauenkirche church and the old mint (now the town hall). Post-Second World War prosperity has brought development of light industry and service sectors. The most notable recent arrival (2002) is Legoland Deutschland, a large theme park south of Günzburg that attracts 1.3 million visitors annually.

Follow gravel track, doglegging L and R over Nau and continue along Danube riverbank passing under road bridge. Before next road bridge, turn L away from river, then R across bridge approach and R again to regain riverbank. Pass **Offingen dam** and hydro-electric power station and dogleg L and R over small stream. Pass under railway bridge and after 700m turn L away from river to reach road. Turn L again, cross railway level crossing and turn second R on cycle track between fields. ▶ Continue onto quiet road, passing bathing beach at **Peterswörthsee** R (accommodation, refreshments). Turn R and R again by tennis club. Follow cycle track under railway and road bridges to reach Stegweide and turn L into **Peterswörth** (38km, 432m).

The cooling towers visible to the right, across fields, are those of Gundremmingen, Germany's largest nuclear power station.

Turn L in middle of village (Peterswörther Strasse) and continue out of village joining cycle track R. Pass series of factories R and opposite entrance to largest of these (a metal extrusion factory), turn L on road under railway bridge (Xaver-Schwarz-Strasse). At T-junction turn R to reach **Gundelfingen station** R. Turn L opposite station (Bahnhofstrasse) and follow road bearing R over

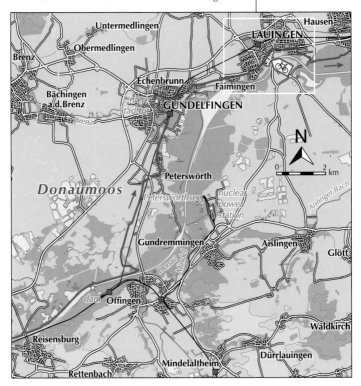

all three branches of River Brenz. Turn L at T-junction (Prof.-Bamann-Strasse) through Untere Stadttor city gate to reach centre of **Gundelfingen** (42km, 438m) (accommodation, refreshments, station).

Gundelfingen (pop. 7750) is situated near the confluence of the rivers Danube and Brenz (three branches of which flow through the town). Its first charter was granted in 1220 and the town developed within town walls and three gates. Part of these walls, the Untere Stadttor city gate and other old buildings are still standing. In 1462 the town, which owed allegiance to the Duke of Bavaria, survived a siege by the forces of the Holy Roman Empire and its citizens were rewarded with taxation privileges by the relieved Duke.

Turn R at T-junction (Hauptstrasse) and R again at end (Lauinger Strasse). Continue out of town over railway

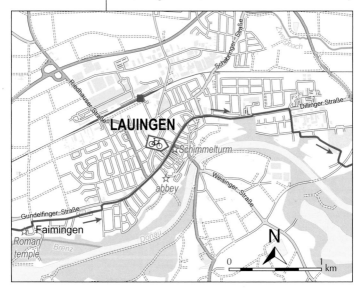

The Apollo Grannus Roman temple in Faimingen

bridge into **Echenbrunn** (accommodation, refreshments). Just before end of village, fork R (Leitenstrasse) and where this ends continue on cycle track between fields into **Faimingen** (refreshments).

Pass through village on Magnus-Scheller-Strasse. ▸ At end turn L (Römerstrasse) and immediately R (Kastellstrasse). Turn L (Friedrich-Ebert-Strasse) and R on cycle lane beside main road (**Gundelfinger Strasse**) then continue along Herzog-Georg-Strasse into Marktplatz in centre of **Lauingen** (47.5km, 441m) (accommodation, refreshments, cycle shop, station).

> **Lauingen** (pop. 11,000) grew as a medieval town around an eighth-century abbey. At its centre, Marktplatz is overlooked by the classical style town hall (1782) and 54m-high Schimmelturm tower (1478). Lauingen's most famous son is St Albertus Magnus (1206–1280). After studying at the University of Padua, he taught at Paris University before founding the University of Köln (1248) and becoming master of the Dominican Order in Germany. He left Köln briefly to become Bishop of Regensburg and later a papal legate,

To the right of the route in Faimingen are the restored remains of Apollo Grannus, the largest Roman temple discovered north of the Alps.

St Albertus Magnus was an all-round renaissance scholar

95

before returning to the university. Although his main teaching was in philosophical theology, he was an all-round scholar who produced works on many subjects including botany, zoology, geography, astronomy and psychology. He was a strong proponent of the value of scientific study alongside theology and was mentor to St Thomas Aquinas.

STAGE 8
Lauingen to Donauwörth

Start	Lauingen Marktplatz (441m)
Finish	Donauwörth town hall (408m)
Distance	41km
Waymarking	Donau Radwanderweg, Deutsche Donau (both inconsistent)

Along this stretch, the Danube continues through a wide agricultural valley, with further areas of fenland to the south. Always away from the river, this stage mostly follows a cycle track beside a main road north of the Danube to Blindheim, where it passes near the site of the Battle of Blindheim (Blenheim). It then crosses the river, following minor roads and field paths to Donauwörth. The stage is generally flat.

Leave **Lauingen Marktplatz** heading NE on Herzog-Georg-Strasse. Continue on **Dillinger Strasse** (cycle track R). Shortly before end of built-up area, turn R at traffic lights (Waihengeyerstrasse). Turn second L (Hergottsruhweg) and R (In der Ludwigsau), bearing L downhill through trees. Bear R before main road, then L to cross this road onto gravel track into forest. Bear L at small clearing, then continue through trees to emerge in grassy area with walk through **footbath**. Turn L uphill and emerge onto residential street (Mozartstrasse). Turn L, then R past St Elisabeth Hospital (Ziegelstrasse) and R

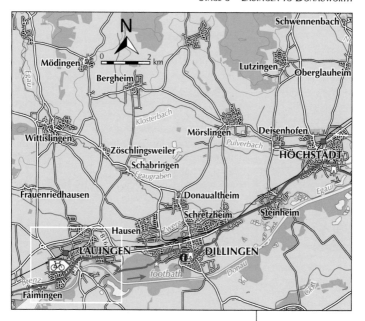

at end into Prälat-Hummel-Strasse. Turn L (Kardinal-von-Waldburg-Strasse), passing former Jesuit university L, and continue on Königstrasse into centre of **Dillingen** (6km, 433m) (accommodation, refreshments, camping, tourist office, cycle shop, station).

map continues
on page 99

> **Dillingen** (pop. 18,000) had its heyday after the Reformation when the Prince Bishop of Augsburg moved his court here (as the town remained Catholic) after Augsburg opted for Protestantism. The castle was remodelled as his residence and a number of churches built, many of which were subsequently redecorated in the rococo style. The former Jesuit university, which has frescoes, ceiling paintings and a golden hall, is now a teacher-training college. The town's attractive main street, Königstrasse,

is lined with 17th- and 18th-century buildings, with Mitteltorturm gateway at one end.

Pass through Mitteltorturm archway and turn R downhill (Am Stadtberg). At roundabout, turn L by taking fourth exit into Kasernplatz. Continue uphill into Am Reitweg and after 600m fork R (Am Galgenberg) passing barracks L. Go over road bridge and turn L into Gutenbergstrasse. Turn R (Rudolf-Diesel-Strasse), alongside main road. After next road junction, join cycle track R of main road and continue for 5km passing through centre of **Steinheim** (10.5km, 422m) (refreshments). ◀ Continue beside main road to reach Marktplatz in centre of **Höchstädt** (13km, 419m) (accommodation, refreshments, station).

This is a busy main road and there is no cycle lane through the village.

Höchstädt (pop. 13,250) grew up beside an important medieval castle perched on a small hill overlooking a bend in the Danube. The original fortress was demolished in the 1580s and replaced with the current Renaissance-style palace as a home for the Duchess of Jülich-Cleves-Berg. The

The palace in Höchstädt has been restored as a state monument

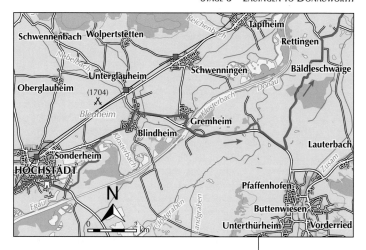

building consists of four almost identical wings, each with a conical corner tower, surrounding a central courtyard. During the Second World War it was used as a depository for cultural artefacts looted from Ukraine and Belarus. Now owned by the Bavarian government as a state monument, it has been extensively renovated.

map continues on page 101

Bear R from Marktplatz into Herzogin-Anna-Strasse, passing **Schloss Höchstädt palace** R. Just after palace bear R onto short cycle track leading to Exerzierplatz. Dogleg L and R at end into Wertinger Strasse and continue on cycle track beside road R. Pass aggregates depot L and after 250m turn L on cycle track beside lagoon. Bear R between fields and continue, circling round more lagoons, to reach **Sonderheim** (17km, 419m) (accommodation, refreshments). Turn R (Hauptstrasse) through village and bear L to reach main road. Turn R and continue on cycle track beside road R to reach **Blindheim** (19km, 417m) (accommodation, station).

The **Battle of Blindheim** (known in English as Blenheim) was a decisive battle fought on 13 August 1704, during the War of the Spanish Succession (1701–1714). It was between 48,000 French and Bavarian troops commanded by the Duke of Tallard, who were marching east to attack Vienna, and 51,000 Alliance troops (English, Dutch, Prussian and Savoyard) commanded by the Duke of Marlborough and Prince Eugene of Savoy. The two armies met on the open plain north-west of Blindheim. The result was a conclusive victory for the Alliance and a rout for France, who lost 30,000 troops (killed, wounded and missing) as well as all their artillery and stores; 6000 were killed and 6500 were wounded on the Alliance side. At the end of the fighting there were over 20,000 bodies on the battlefield and, 300 years later, farmers still unearth remains. In England, a grateful Queen Anne rewarded Marlborough with a stately home, Blenheim palace, named after the battle.

To visit Blenheim battlefield site, turn L (Oberfeldweg) off Bahnhofstrasse and continue through fields to reach battle monument after 1.5km.

Cycle through village on Höchstädtler Strasse and continue onto Bahnhofstrasse. ◀ Turn R (Mühlstrasse), heading out of village and join cycle track L of road. Fork L (Hauptstrasse) into **Gremheim** (21.5km, 415m) (accommodation).

Continue on road bearing R to circle through village. Just after end of village bear L onto cycle track towards Danube and climb up to cross river on cycle track L of main road. Continue on cycle track beside road until it ends after 2.5km. Bear L through fields, turning R by Ruppenmühle mill to return to road. Continue alongside main road until next road junction and turn sharply L onto side road. Follow this road for 5km winding through fields and passing **Bäldleschwaige** farm R (accommodation, refreshments) to reach **Rettingen** (32.5km, 402m).

Just before Rettingen, turn sharply R onto another side road and follow this to **Zusum** (37km, 401m) (accommodation). Continue on road through village and after 1km turn L on short unsurfaced cycle track leading

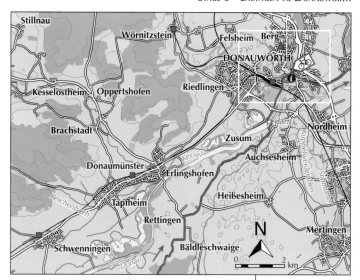

to Danube (this can be muddy after rain). Turn R along riverbank and turn L to cross river on **dam** of Donauwörth hydro-electric power station. Continue away from river for 100m and turn R on road (Am Kesseldamm). Continue

Rieder Tor gateway connects Ried island and Donauwörth

101

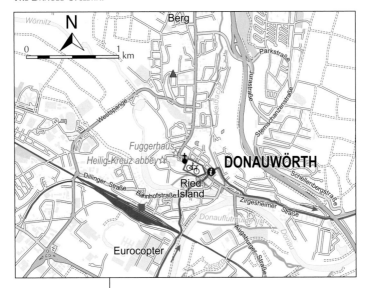

under road bridge onto Industriestrasse and pass **Airbus Eurocopter factory** L.

Continue under railway bridge into Gartenstrasse and turn R (Bahnhofstrasse) at T-junction. Turn L (Hindenburgerstrasse) over Wörnitz river onto **Ried island** and continue through pedestrian precinct. Cross pedestrian bridge over second arm of Wörnitz and through Rieder Tor medieval archway into centre of **Donauwörth** (41km, 408m) (accommodation, refreshments, YH, tourist office, cycle shop, station).

DONAUWÖRTH

Donauwörth (pop. 18,250) is situated at the confluence of the Danube and Wörnitz rivers and was the point where the imperial road from Nuremburg to Augsburg crossed the Danube. The oldest part is on the small Ried island, nowadays an area of bars and cafés outside the town walls. From the island, Rieder Tor, one of four original gateways, leads through the city walls to the main medieval city on the north side of the Wörnitz. The main street (Reichsstrasse) runs uphill from the historic town hall and the Hall of the Teutonic Knights at the bottom, past other old buildings including the customs house. Further up are the 15th-century Gothic Liebenfrauenmünster parish church and 16th-century Renaissance Fuggerhaus, once owned by the Fugger family of financiers from Augsburg and now the seat of the regional government. At the top is Heilig-Kreuz Benedictine abbey, which was founded in the 11th century and originally built to hold an alleged piece of the true cross, acquired during the crusades. The present building dates from the late 17th to early 18th centuries. Religious tensions that were to lead to the Thirty Years' War first came to a head in Donauwörth, where riots between Protestants and Catholics in 1606 were the precursor to a war that eventually killed eight million people.

STAGE 9
Donauwörth to Ingolstadt

Start	Donauwörth town hall (408m)
Finish	Ingolstadt, footbridge (367m)
Distance	59.5km
Waymarking	Donau Radwanderweg, Deutsches Donau

This long stage, mostly away from the Danube, at first follows cycle tracks beside main roads as the route undulates through the foothills of the Fränkische Alb. A long section on field tracks and minor roads comes next before the Danube is crossed to the stunning Renaissance town of Neuburg. From here the route, now completely flat, skirts the wooded wetland flood plain of the river to reach the city of Ingolstadt.

From outside **Donauwörth town hall**, head NE along Rathausgasse and where this turns L continue ahead on cycle track through narrow blue archway and over river Kaibach. Turn R along Promenade taking L of two tracks

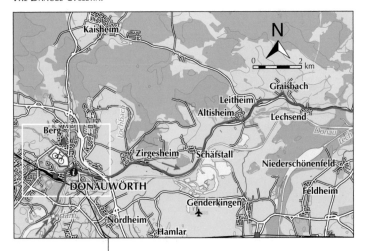

and bear L to pass under bridge. Cross a road and continue through car park to emerge alongside main road. Bear L on cycle track beside **Zirgesheimer Strasse**, soon crossing to R, and continue out of town under motorway bridge to pass **Zirgesheim** (3km, 400m) L (accommodation, refreshments).

Just before end of village, cycle track crosses to L of road and continues for 4.5km. Just after sports club R, fork L uphill on Gartenstrasse. Turn R (Willibaldstrasse) to reach centre of **Altisheim** (8.5km, 413m) (accommodation, refreshments).

Turn L onto main road (Donaustrasse) and at end of village join cycle track R. Continue uphill into **Leitheim** (9.5km, 453m). In centre of village, opposite the Schloss and ornate Schlosskirche castle church, turn L (Jurastrasse) and immediately R (An der Leiten). Continue ahead on cycle track heading downhill to main road. Fork L (Hartnitstrasse) into **Graisbach** (11km, 407m) (accommodation, refreshments). At bottom of hill turn R (Graf-Reisach-Strasse) back to main road and follow this uphill (cycle track L) to **Lechsend** (12km, 432m). Cycle through village on road and rejoin cycle track, now on R,

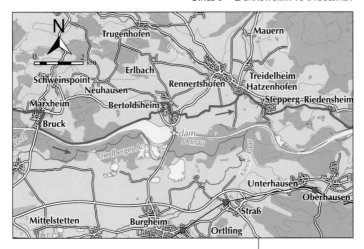

climbing over a low ridge to reach **Marxheim** (14.5km, 402m) (accommodation, refreshments).

map continues
on page 106

Turn R in centre of village (Donaustrasse) and follow this (cycle track appearing R) towards hamlet of **Bruck** (accommodation, refreshments). ▶ Just before Bruck, turn L and immediately bear R on gravel track winding past tennis courts to reach riverbank. Turn L on cycle track below flood dyke for 5km. Where river widens into lake above dam, fork L on road away from river. Cross main road and turn L (Lichtengasse). At end, turn R uphill winding through centre of **Bertoldsheim** (21.5km, 397m) (accommodation, refreshments).

Fork R (Am Schlossberg) past St Michael's church L. Fork R by a restaurant and turn L just before Schloss Bertoldsheim. After 150m fork R (An der Allee). Cross main road and follow quiet road winding between fields for 3km to reach edge of **Hatzenhofen** (25.5km, 389m) (accommodation, refreshments).

Cross stream and turn R at T-junction (Egloffstrasse). Continue out of village on Hatzenhofener Strasse. Fork R (Usselstrasse) then bear L and L again to reach centre of **Stepperg** (accommodation, refreshments).

Just upstream of Bruck is the confluence of Danube and Lech, a major tributary that rises in the Austrian Tirol and flows down through Augsburg.

Turn R (Rennertshofener Strasse) and continue on Antonibergstrasse bearing L opposite entrance to Stepperg Schloss (still Antonibergstrasse). Where this turns R, continue ahead on cycle track uphill through avenue of trees and into woods. After emerging from trees, bear R on road through fields and emerge onto road (Hartlweg) into **Riedensheim** (29.5km, 400m).

Turn R at T-junction (Auenstrasse) and follow this bearing R out of village. Immediately after village turn L on cycle track through fields to reach Danube. Turn L below flood dyke for 750m with Finkenstein hill rising L. Bear L away from river to follow cycle track winding through fields. Bear L on road (Eulatalstrasse) leading into **Bittenbrunn** (34km, 386m) (accommodation, refreshments). Turn R on main road (**Monheimer Strasse**) joining cycle track R to pass **Laisacker** L (accommodation).

Continue into built-up area and turn R (Ingolstadter Strasse) crossing Danube on Elisenbrücke bridge into **Neuburg** (36km, 384m) (accommodation, refreshments, camping, tourist office, cycle shop, station).

map continues on page 109

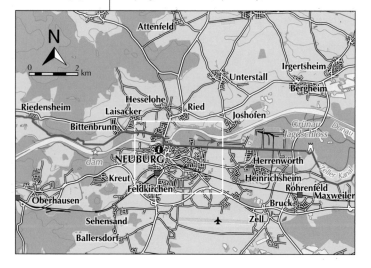

Schlosskapelle ceiling in Neuburg makes quite an impression

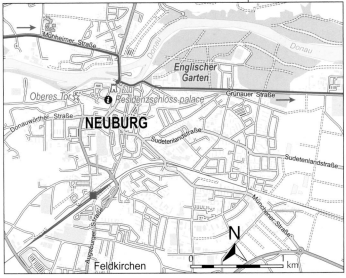

The oldest and prettiest part of **Neuburg** (pop. 28,750), Obere Stadt, sits atop the Stadtberg, a small hill beside the Danube. The town is dominated by the Italianate-style Residenzschloss palace, which was built in the early 16th century for the ruler Count Ottheinrich when the town became capital of the newly established state of Pfalz-Neuburg. Other important buildings include the oldest Protestant church in Bavaria, Schlosskapelle (1543), which is nicknamed 'the Bavarian Sistine' – an allusion to its highly decorated ceiling frescoes, which are said to rival those in Rome's Sistine chapel. Karlsplatz, the main square of Obere Stadt, is lined by restored historic houses and the domed copper cupola of the Hofkirche church. Further west is the Oberes Tor, a twin-towered 16th-century city gate. Count Ottheinrich was also responsible for building Grünau Jagdschloss hunting lodge, 6km east of Neuburg, which is passed after leaving town.

To reach Obere Stadt, continue ahead through gate.

Immediately over bridge, turn R (Elisenplatz) with Unteres Tor city gate ahead. ◄ Turn R before the gate (Zur Holle) and immediately R again downhill through an archway to pass under bridge. Continue beside river on Oskar-Wittmann-Strasse then bear away from river (**Grünauer Strasse**) on cycle track L of road. Continue for 5km with sprawling wooded area of the **Englischer Garten** L and continue past **Herrenwörth** (39.5km, 379m) R and industrial area L. At roundabout continue straight ahead to reach **Grünau Jagdschloss** (old hunting lodge). Pass lodge L, then turn L and R onto tree-lined avenue to reach **Rohrenfeld** (43.5km, 378m) (station). Fork L on another tree-lined avenue and after 500m turn L onto gravel track winding through fields.

The barrier defaults to closed position. To raise it, press the small handle on the left of the road.

Turn R into woods and follow winding track through forest. Emerge onto road and cross level crossing. ◄ Turn L (Am Anger) into **Weichering** (49km, 376m) (accommodation, refreshments, station). At T-junction turn L (Kapellenplatz) passing St Antonius chapel R then continue into Achstrasse and bear R (Bahnhofstrasse). Pass

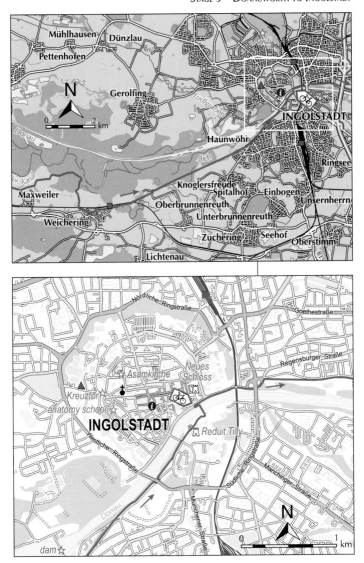

station L and continue ahead through woods. Pass under railway bridge and continue to Rosenschwaig. At road junction, bear L over bridge and R on track parallel to stream for 4km to reach the suburbs of Ingolstadt at **Haunwöhr** (56km, 369m).

Continue on cycle track under road bridge then fork L following riverbank track. Cross approach road to next bridge. After passing extensive defensive bastions including **Reduit Tilly** R, bear R and turn L to cross Danube footbridge into **Ingolstadt** (59.5km, 367m) (accommodation, refreshments, camping, YH, tourist office, cycle shop, station).

INGOLSTADT

Ingolstadt (pop. 127,000) has an old historic centre contained within the remnants of ancient bastions, surrounded by one of Germany's most dynamic and prosperous modern cities. At the city's heart, the *altstadt* (old town) contains a number of important buildings including the French-influenced Neues Schloss (nowadays the Bavarian army museum) and Liebfrauenmünster cathedral, both constructed during the early 15th century. The crowning jewel is the rococo Maria de Victoria church (also known as Asamkirche – named after its designers, the Asam brothers). Built between 1732 and 1736, the church has a trompe l'oeil ceiling that is the world's largest flat-surface fresco, and a side chapel containing the Lepanto monstrance with a gold and silver depiction of the battle of Lepanto (1571). The Kreuztor gateway (1385), one of two remaining city gates, has been adopted as the emblem of Ingolstadt. The old school of anatomy within the university was chosen by Mary Shelley as the setting for her best-selling novel *Frankenstein*.

The city's modern prosperity arises from its two oil refineries as well as it being the headquarters of the car manufacturer Audi, which has its main offices, factory and motor museum just north of the city. There are also four breweries, and local beer connoisseurs take pride in the fact that in 1516 a decree was issued in Ingolstadt that governed the purity of beer in Bavaria. This was eventually adopted by the whole of Germany and is still in force today.

The old anatomy school in Ingolstadt, 'birthplace' of Frankenstein

STAGE 10

Ingolstadt to Kelheim

Start	Ingolstadt, footbridge (367m)
Finish	Kelheim quayside (344m)
Distance	50km (45.5km cycling; 4.5km ferry)
Waymarking	Donau Radweg, Deutsche Donau

This stage passes at first through a wide flat valley, using quiet roads, field tracks and riverside paths to reach Vohburg and Neustadt. Towards the end, the limestone foothills of the Fränkische Alb are reached before Weltenburg. Where the Danube has cut a sheer-sided gorge through these hills, with no room for riverside tracks, frequent boats can be taken through the gorge to Kelheim. The going is flat except for an ascent between Eining and Weltenburg.

From N end of Danube **footbridge** in Ingolstadt, follow cycle track between **Schlosslände** L and river R heading E. Pass under railway and road bridges and turn R (Gerhart-Hauptmann-Strasse). Continue ahead across Kurt-Huber-Strasse to pass between sports centre L and car park R. Dogleg under motorway bridge and continue on cycle track along flood dyke passing sewerage works

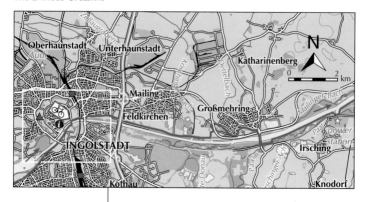

and power station L. Turn L beyond electricity sub-station. At T-junction, turn L on winding cycle track between trees and lagoon. Dogleg R and L across entrance to industrial estate. Turn sharply R under main road to reach Nibelungenstrasse and turn R past **Grossmehring** (8km, 361m) L (accommodation, refreshments, cycle shop).

By St Michaels church L, fork R (Uferstrasse) alongside an old Danube bend R, now a lagoon. At end, turn R and immediately R again. Continue over main road beside roundabout and fork immediately L on narrow track to cross road bridge over Danube. At end of bridge, turn L across road to follow gravel track into woods. After 500m, zigzag L and R to reach riverbank then continue beside river for 4.5km, passing power station R, to reach **Vohburg dam**. ◄

Turn R on track from dam, cross side stream and turn L on cycle track along flood dyke to reach **Vohburg bridge** (16.5km, 356m) (accommodation, refreshments, tourist office, cycle shop).

Vohburg (pop. 7500) is a medieval town that grew up around a castle atop a small hill just south of the Danube. The castle was destroyed by Swedish troops during the Thirty Years' War, but nearly 500m of wall and a number of gateways, including the Burgtor main gate, have been restored.

The track past the power station can be muddy when wet.

*Agnes Bernauer,
secret wife of the
Duke of Bavaria's son,
was drowned in 1435*

The most well-known resident of the castle was Agnes Bernauer, a commoner who secretly married the son of the Duke of Bavaria in 1432 against his father's wishes. They lived in Vohburg for three years until their secret was discovered, after which she was taken to Straubing and drowned as a witch on orders of the Duke. Her sad fate has been immortalised in a story by Friedrich Hebbel and a musical composition by Carl Orff.

map continues
on page 115

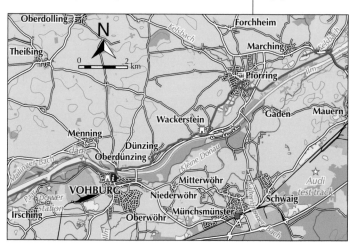

Turn L over Danube and R on opposite bank (Schützenstrasse), with cycle track (a stretch of old road) L. Bear L (Dorfstrasse) into **Dünzing** (18.5km, 358m) (accommodation, refreshments). Turn sharp R in village (still Dorfstrasse) and leave village bearing R (Dünziger Strasse) between fields. Continue on Vohburger Strasse (staying off main road) into **Wackerstein** (21km, 360m) (refreshments). Bear R past attractively decorated restaurant L. Turn L alongside main road and fork L following quiet road out of village through fields, passing lagoons R to enter **Pförring** (24km, 353m) on Ingolstadter Strasse.

At T-junction turn R over stream (an old Danube course) into Donaustrasse and turn third L. Bear R (Geisgries) and follow this street bearing L out of village past lagoon L. Cross main road and continue on cycle track through woods. Turn L along Danube flood dyke for 3km.

Pass under road bridge and bear L, then turn L and L again to cross Danube (cycle track L). Continue alongside road for 600m then turn L at road junction (Donaustrasse) to continue beside road (cycle track L) into **Neustadt** (31km, 351m) (accommodation, refreshments, camping, cycle shop, station).

Neustadt (pop. 13,000) has a medieval old town within the clearly defined outlines of a rectangular city wall now planted with trees to form Kastanienallee. Surrounding this, the new town and surrounding districts have seen substantial population growth (from 4000 in 1972), with many people being employed by companies producing automotive parts for Audi and BMW. Audi has an extensive test track 5km from Neustadt.

At road junction, where main road bears R into town centre, fork L (Bad Gögginger Strasse). This road becomes Neustädter Strasse to enter **Bad Gögging** (33km, 357m) (accommodation, refreshments, tourist office, cycle shop).

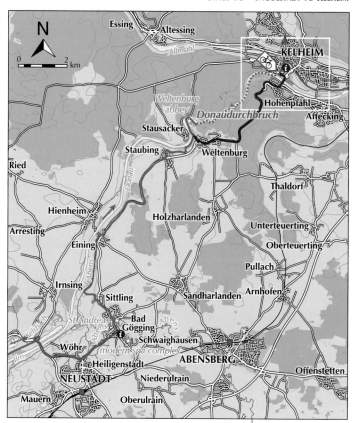

Bad Gögging is a spa town with sulphur springs that was first developed by the Romans. The location of the original spa was subsequently lost and St Andreas church was built over the site. In the late 19th century, new baths opened and these have developed into an extensive spa complex, with a variety of treatment and rehabilitation facilities available, as well as hotels and a golf course.

Cross river Abens and continue through town on Römerstrasse to reach **Sittling** (34km, 358m). Just before church turn L (sp Sittling 200-). Turn R at T-junction and continue past hop gardens. Cross first flood dyke and turn R along second dyke. Pass Roman fort (Kastell Abusina) R then turn R over small bridge and immediately L to reach **Eining** (37.5km, 350m). ◄ Turn R uphill (Zur Überfuhr) to reach main road and turn L (Abusinastrasse). Follow road for 5km climbing over low ridge to reach beginning of **Staubing**. Turn L at crossroads (Sandharlandener Strasse) then bear L to wind through village on Ortsring, passing church R. Fork L at T-junction (Am Krautgarten) to continue between fields. Turn L before reaching main road onto gravel track leading to Danube. Turn R along riverbank to emerge on riverside road (Asamstrasse) by large car park, with **Weltenburg** R (accommodation, refreshments). Turn L to reach **Kloster Weltenburg abbey** (45km, 349m).

A track continues alongside the Danube to Weltenburg. This is very rough in places and is not recommended.

First founded in AD620, **Kloster Weltenburg abbey** is considered the oldest abbey in Bavaria. Its baroque cloisters surround St Georgenkirche church, a masterpiece built by the Asam brothers from 1716 to 1739. The abbey's first foundation was dissolved in 1803 during the Napoleonic War. Reformed in 1842 as a Benedictine subsidiary house to Metten abbey, it became a fully independent Benedictine abbey in 1913. Within the abbey is a brewery that has operated since 1050, making it the oldest monastic brewery in the world. A range of beers is produced, the best-known being a dark beer called Kloster Barock dunkel. These beverages can be sampled at a large restaurant and beer garden on the premises.

Between Weltenburg and Kelheim the Danube flows through the Donaudurchbruch, a rugged gorge with neither roads nor tracks following the river. The most popular way to reach Kelheim, and that giving the best views, is to embark on one of the frequent boats that traverse the gorge.

A view of Kelheim seen from Befreiungshalle

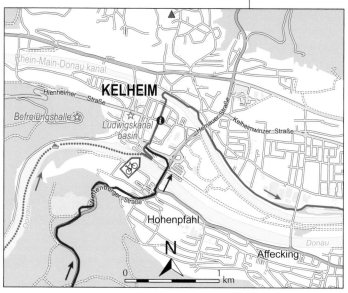

Alternative route avoiding the Donaudurchbruch
To carry on cycling and avoid the boat trip along the Donaudurchbruch gorge, return to **Weltenburg** then turn L through village, following road uphill through woodland (ascending 150m) before descending to reach **Kelheim bridge**. Cross bridge (cycle track L) then bear L off bridge into Bahnhofstrasse. Turn R onto Donaustrasse, joining Stage 11.

For the main route, continue on riverside cycle track for 400m to reach pontoon (45.5km, 344m) where frequent boats depart through Donaudurchbruch gorge to reach **Kelheim** (50km, 344m) (accommodation, refreshments, YH, tourist office, cycle shop).

KELHEIM

Kelheim (pop. 15,500) sits astride a peninsula between the Danube and Altmühl rivers. King Ludwig I left his mark on the town with two major constructions: a massive monument and an ill-fated canal. The *Befreiungshalle* (Hall of Liberation) sits on a bluff high above the river. Commissioned by Ludwig to celebrate German liberation from Napoleon, and built by Leo von Klenze, it takes the form of a cylindrical drum, with buttresses dividing it into 18 panels. Inside it contains 34 enormous winged angels with hands joined, an allegory to the individual German states coming together to defeat Napoleon at the battle of Leipzig on 18 October 1813. It opened 50 years after the battle. The Ludwigskanal was an early attempt to connect the Rhine and Danube basins by canal. Opened in 1846, it was a narrow canal with 100 locks. From the outset, providing a water supply to the higher stages proved difficult and the canal proved very expensive to operate. It was abandoned in 1950 after damage incurred in the Second World War proved too costly to repair. The old quays and locks at the canal entrance remain in the centre of Kelheim.

The 171km-long Rhein–Main–Donau Canal connects the Rhine basin in north-west mainland Europe with that of the Danube in south-east Europe, enabling boats to cross the continent from the North Sea to the Black Sea. A successor to Ludwigskanal and a triumph of engineering, it was opened in 1992 after many years of debate, planning and construction. En route from Bamberg, on the river Main, to Kelheim, where it joins the Danube, the canal crosses the European watershed at an altitude of 406m, the highest point on earth reachable by ocean-going vessels. By 2005 the canal was carrying over 7.5 million tonnes annually, mostly bulk goods such as animal feeds, timber, scrap metal, fertilizers and aggregates, although this has fallen with the economic downturn in Europe. While it was being constructed, the canal encountered much environmental opposition, but this was assuaged by substantial expenditure on projects to ameliorate the environmental impact. The resulting water-borne tonnage saves over 250,000 truck trips by road every year, a clear environmental benefit.

STAGE 11
Kelheim to Regensburg

Start	Kelheim quayside (344m)
Finish	Regensburg, Brückturm (340m)
Distance	37.5km
Waymarking	Donau Radweg, Deutsche Donau

This stage brings with it a change of scenery as the Danube cuts its way through the foothills of the Fränkische Alb. The route, completely flat, stays beside the river, closely following every bend until emerging into Regensburg, one of Europe's best-preserved medieval cities.

From **Kelheim quayside**, take ramp R and L up to car park. Turn R through car park and go across main road into Donaustrasse. ▶ Pass through Donautor gateway and continue along cobbled street. Cross Ludwigsplatz ahead into Altmühlstrasse and go through Altmühltor gateway to reach Altmühl River. Bear L on modern suspension bridge curving over river. At end of bridge, continue ahead along upper level of flood dyke and after 50m drop down L onto Friedhofstrasse. Turn R to reach Altmühl riverbank and bear L beside river. Continue out

Alternative route avoiding the Donaudurchbruch in Stage 10 rejoins main route here.

of town under road bridge. Follow cycle track along flood dyke R of road passing under another road bridge. After 3km pass **Kelheimwinzer** (5km, 345m) (accommodation, refreshments).

Fork R to pass under road bridge, then turn R and L onto flood dyke. Continue to **Herrnsaal** (camping), where track turns L briefly away from river into edge of village. Turn R (Stiftstrasse) and after 100m turn R back to riverbank.

After 3km emerge onto main road and follow this until it turns away from river towards **Kapfelberg** (accommodation) on hillside L. Turn R (Am Jachthafen) beside lagoon to reach Kapfelberg marina (12km, 339m) (camping).

Continue on road following river for 2km, then follow road away from river. At crossroads, turn R under railway bridge (Dorfstrasse) into **Poikam** (14km, 343m) (station). Turn R (Zur Donaubrücke), then R again to cross Danube over **Poikam dam**. At crossroads after bridge turn R (Industriestrasse), then R again back under bridge. Immediately under bridge, turn R onto cycle track away from river passing behind riding stables, following this as it curves L beside road. Continue along riverside, passing two huge **stone lions** and a cliffside memorial to the opening of the road in 1794. Where main road turns away from river, bear L on riverside cycle track passing **Bad Abbach** (17.5km, 337m) R (accommodation, refreshments).

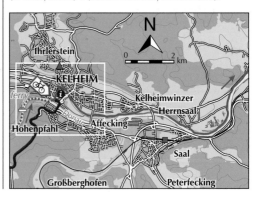

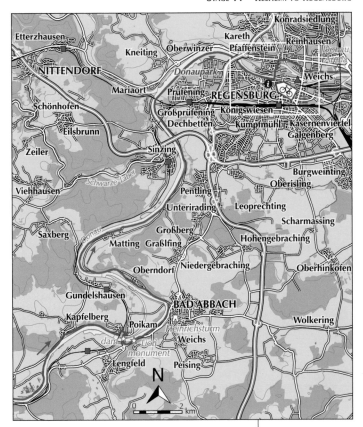

Bad Abbach (pop. 11,500) is another spa town with sulphurous springs. First recorded in 1262, by the 15th century the spring water was believed to cure rheumatic diseases. The town was frequented by royalty in the 18th century, and the original spa buildings were constructed in 1872. The spa was operated by the Bavarian Red Cross from 1949 to 2004, during which time it fell into financial difficulty. Since 2004, however, new owners have

This lion memorial near Bad Abbach commemorates building the riverside road in 1794

built more facilities and increased the services offered. The most significant building in town is the Heinrichsturm, a 27m-tall tower with masonry 4.5m thick. Apart from a few foundations this is all that remains of a castle that was already partly in ruins by the 15th century, but was finally destroyed by Swedish forces during the Thirty Years' War.

Continue under modern single stay pedestrian bridge and rejoin riverside road. Continue through **Oberndorf** (19.5km, 337m) (accommodation, refreshments). After village, bear L onto riverside cycle track and follow this into **Matting** (24km, 338m) (refreshments). Pass cable operated pedestrian ferry L and turn L (An der Donau), passing church R. At end of village bear L onto riverside cycle track. Continue past **Unterirading** (accommodation, refreshments) and under motorway and railway bridges. Pass **Grossprüfening** (31km, 335m) (refreshments), where track doglegs around ferry ramp, and continue under another railway bridge. Cycle track now follows river as it makes a long sweeping bend around **Regensburg**.

Pass **Donaupark** and continue under motorway bridge. Dogleg R and L by **Regensburg dam** to continue along riverbank. Emerge onto Holzländestrasse passing footbridge L. Fork R into Keplerstrasse, becoming Fischmarkt and then Goldene-Bären-Strasse. The stage ends by **Brückturm**

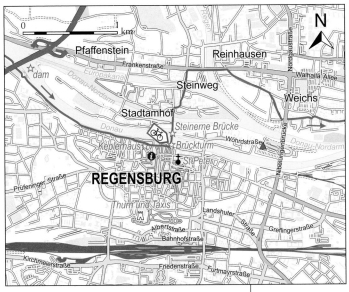

Steinerne Brücke in Regensburg is one of the oldest bridges over the Danube

bridge tower (37.5km, 340m) of **Regensburg Steinerne Brücke bridge** (accommodation, refreshments, YH, camping, tourist office, cycle shop, station).

REGENSBURG

Regensburg (pop. 136,000), which stands at the most northerly point reached by the Danube, is regarded as one of Europe's best-preserved medieval cities thanks to its mass of tiny alleyways and attractive squares. The Romans built a large fort here as a base for legions controlling the northern borders of their empire. When the Romans left, Regensburg became capital of Bavaria from AD530 to 1245, after which it became a self-governing free city within the Holy Roman Empire. With the redrawing of European boundaries following the collapse of the HRE during the Napoleonic War, the city lost its independence and became part of the Bavarian Kingdom in 1810. It has remained Bavarian ever since.

Many historical buildings can be found in the altstadt, which is a UNESCO-listed heritage site. The *Steinerne Brücke* (stone bridge), built in 1146, was the first bridge over this section of the Danube and it resulted in the city becoming a transport and trading hub on the route between Italy and central Europe. The merchants' houses, with characteristic towers, reflected this importance.

The spires of Dom St Peter cathedral soar above the old town. The building of this great Gothic cathedral began in 1255, based on an older structure (a small part of which remains). Primarily a vanity project, intended to demonstrate the wealth of the newly independent city, work continued for 300 years until it was halted by lack of funds in 1525. The cathedral was not finally completed until 1869. The large number of religious buildings in the altstadt led Goethe to comment: *here, churches stand on churches*.

By contrast, the Schloss Thurn und Taxis – built in 1812 inside a former abbey – was a thoroughly modern (at the time of its construction) palace. Built for the Prince of Thurn und Taxis, and paid for by the profit he made by selling the rights to a European postal monopoly that his family had owned since the 15th century, it had flowing hot water, central heating and exquisite interiors. Although it is still the family residence today, it can be visited.

Among Regensburg's notable residents, Johannes Kepler (1571–1630) was best known for establishing knowledge on the orbits of the planets. His house (Keplerstrasse 5) is now a museum. Joseph Ratzinger, who went on to become Pope Benedict XVI, was professor of theology at Regensburg University from 1969 to 1977.

STAGE 12
Regensburg to Straubing

Start	Regensburg, Brückturm (340m)
Finish	Straubing, Theresienplatz (337m)
Distance	53.5km
Waymarking	Donau Radweg

The Danube, suddenly busy with shipping, turns to head southeast, meandering along the northern edge of the Gäuboden plain with the foothills of the Bayerischer Wald forest rising to the north. The route, almost entirely flat, mostly follows the riverbank or flood dykes near the river, with some use of field paths and quiet country roads. One of the most ostentatious monuments on the Danube, King Ludwig's Walhalla, is passed after Donaustauf.

From corner of Goldene-Bären-Strasse by **Brückturm** in Regensburg, head N across Danube on Steinerne Brücke bridge. Continue into Am Brückenbasar square and turn R (Andreasstrasse). Bear L onto Protzenweiherbrücke (cycle lane R) over canal lock to reach major road junction. Turn R on cycle track beside road (Frankenstrasse) and cross

map continues on page 128

River Regen. Fork R (Holzgartenstrasse) and after 500m fork R again (Bedelgasse). Turn L (Johannisstrasse) under road bridge. At end, turn L (Gärtnerstrasse) and immediately R (Schwabelweiser Weg) then follow this dogleg-ging L and R between houses out of Regensburg.

Continue on cycle track beside field and go under rail-way bridge. Follow asphalt track below flood dyke, climb briefly onto dyke to pass under road bridge then return to asphalt road through **Schwabelweis** (accommodation, refreshments). Turn R onto riverside cycle track and continue past **Tegernheim** L (6.5km, 329m) (accommodation, refresh-ments), with Walhalla visible on hillside ahead. Continue following flood dyke passing **Donaustauf** L (9.5km, 328m) (accommodation, refreshments, tourist office).

Donaustauf (pop. 3750) is a market town clus-tered around a small hill topped by a ruined castle that was the country home of the Prince of Thurn und Taxis until it was destroyed by fire in 1880. A Chinese pagoda below the hill was moved to Regensburg after the fire, but was returned to Donaustauf in 1999.

The imposing classical temple, **Walhalla**, is found on a hilltop beside the Danube, just downstream from Donaustauf. It is a reproduction of the Athenian Parthenon and was commissioned by King Ludwig I as a pantheon for Germanic heroes. Leo von Klenze designed it, and it opened in 1842. Made of marble, with 348 marble steps leading to the entrance, it contains 130 marble busts and 65 plaques commemorating the great and the good of Germanic-speaking peoples. While many are obvi-ously German (including Beethoven, Bismarck, Goethe, Gutenberg, Handel, Luther, Schiller, Wagner and, of course, King Ludwig I himself), others have tenuous German connections. These include three English kings (two Saxons, Alfred the Great and his grandfather Egbert, as well as William III of Orange), the Venerable Bede and a number of

Flemish painters including van Dyck and Rubens. The name Walhalla originates from the place where Wotan, leader of the gods in Nordic legend, welcomed new entrants into heaven.

Walhalla is a pantheon commemorating 195 'Germanic' heroes

Bear L under road bridge and pass road leading L to **Walhalla**. ▶ Continue on riverside cycle track below Walhalla. Continue on past **Sulzbach**, then bear R away from road following flood dyke beside river to reach **Demling** (14.5km, 325m).

To visit Walhalla by cycle, turn L and follow signs forking R uphill. Alternatively, continue on riverbank, leave your cycle and follow footpath uphill.

Continue along flood dyke, passing **Bach** (accommodation, refreshments) and **Frengkofen** (18.5km, 328m) (accommodation, refreshments). The south-facing hillside on the left of the Danube, from Bach to Wörth, is part of Germany's smallest wine growing region, which produces mainly dry white table wine. Pass under motorway bridge and immediately bear L to pass through **Kiefenholz** (22km, 325m) (refreshments). ▶

Kiefenholz can be bypassed by continuing along riverbank on unpaved track (Über Donauschleife).

Before end of village, turn R back to riverbank (sp Kleinkiefenholz) and continue past **Geisling dam**. Where road turns L, continue ahead on unpaved cycle track

127

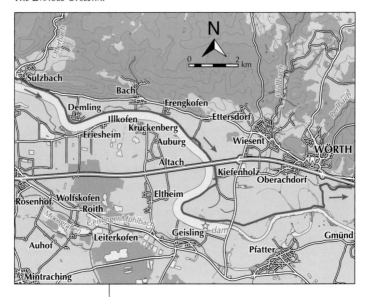

along flood dyke passing under road bridge. After 4.5km, turn L opposite a picnic area on quiet road winding through fields, with **Schloss Wörth** palace visible ahead, to reach another flood dyke.

Turn R onto winding track beside dyke, then L at next crossroads on bridge over Wiesent stream. Turn R on cycle track parallel with motorway. At crossing of tracks cycle ahead up a small rise and continue between fields. Turn L at next junction, then turn R and L over wider road. Continue straight ahead through fields for 3km, parallel with motorway 250m away L. Turn R at third crossroads to reach **Pondorf** (39km, 329m) (refreshments).

Turn L after church (Donaugasse) downhill to reach Danube and turn L on unpaved track along flood dyke R of road. Emerge onto quiet road and bear L through fields to reach **Pittrich** (45km, 319m). Turn L, over bridge and continue through fields and over Kössnach stream into **Kössnach** (47.5km, 322m) (accommodation, refreshments).

Go ahead at crossroads (Wirtsgasse), then turn R at T-junction (Straubinger Strasse) and continue out of village. Where this road turns away from river into Unterzeitldorn, bear R on cycle track alongside flood dyke and continue between main road L and Danube R. Pass under main road and emerge onto village street (An der Kössnach) into **Sossau** (50km, 318m) (refreshments).

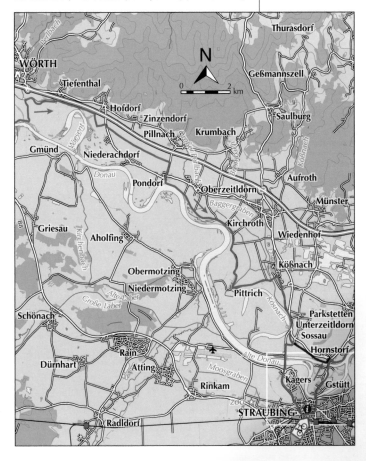

Shortcut avoiding Straubing

To bypass Straubing, go straight ahead at end of village beside flood dyke to reach **Hornstorf** after 1.75km. Bear L, parallel to main road, and continue ahead to reach round-about. Cross side road and after 25m turn L away from main road, following cycle track curving L through under-pass. Emerge onto Ziererstrasse to continue on Stage 13.

For the main route, turn R over drainage canal, then L on cycle track beside main road (cycle track L).

Cross **Straubing dam** and continue beside main road (Westtangente), passing **Kagers** and Gäubodenvolksfest grounds (both L), to reach beginning of Straubing. Climb gently uphill and turn L into **Theresienplatz** in centre of **Straubing** (53.5km, 337m) (accommodation, refreshments, YH, camping, tourist office, cycle shop, station).

Theresienplatz in Straubing with Holy trinity column and Stadtturm tower

Straubing (pop. 45,000) is the main town of the Gäuboden region and the site of the Gäubodenvolksfest, Bavaria's second largest

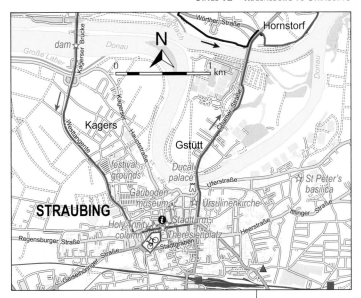

annual beer festival after the Munich Oktoberfest. Lasting for 11 days during the middle of August, it attracts 1.5 million visitors who consume 750,000 litres of locally brewed beer in six enormous beer tents seating 25,000 people. Other attractions include the world's largest movable roller-coaster and a parade.

The town itself was originally another Roman settlement (there is a Roman collection in the Gäubodenmuseum that includes a number of golden helmets), which was established as a medieval town in 1218. The main square (Theresienplatz) is lined by pastel-coloured late 14th-century houses and overlooked by the Stadtturm city watch tower, town hall and golden *Dreifaltigkeitssäule* (Holy Trinity column). The exuberant Ursulinenkirche was the last church designed by the Asam brothers.

Gäuboden museum in Straubing has a collection of golden Roman helmets

131

STAGE 13
Straubing to Deggendorf

Start	Straubing, Theresienplatz (337m)
Finish	Deggendorf, Hans-Krämer-Strasse (312m)
Distance	39km
Waymarking	Donau Radweg

The Danube continues flowing along the northern edge of the fertile Gäuboden plain. The wooded slopes of the Bayerisher Wald are off to the left, with occasional outliers coming close to the river, particularly around Bogen. The route, generally flat, mostly follows the Danube flood dyke along the northern bank, either close to or right beside the river.

map continues on page 134

Head E along Ludwigsplatz (the continuation of **Theresienplatz**) in Straubing and turn L at end into Stadtgraben. Pass **Ducal palace** L and cross Danube. Continue on **Chamer Strasse** (cycle track R) through

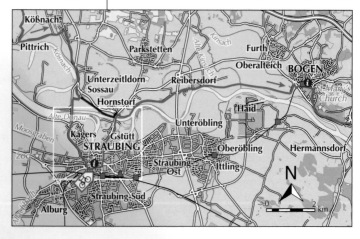

Gstütt (refreshments, camping, cycle shop). Cross navigable channel into **Hornstorf** (2.5km, 317m) and turn R into Ziererstrasse. ▶ Follow this quiet road, bearing L alongside flood dyke. Bear L again away from river, passing under road bridge into **Reibersdorf** (6km, 317m) (accommodation, refreshments).

Alternative route avoiding Straubing in Stage 12 rejoins main route here.

Turn R and L (Donaustrasse), passing church R, alongside river. Bear R on road alongside flood dyke and follow this for 3.5km. Bear L past tennis club, then sharply R on cycle track alongside Kinsach stream. Turn L over bridge, parallel with railway, then R (Bahnhofstrasse) over level crossing past station L. Cross Bogenbach stream and turn R into Stadtplatz in centre of **Bogen** (12km, 320m) (accommodation, refreshments, tourist office, cycle shop, station).

Bogen (pop. 10,000) sits beside the Bogenberg hill, which rises over 100m above the Danube east of the town. On top of the hill is a church that has for many centuries been a centre of pilgrimage. Beside the high altar are two images of Mary – one from the 13th century and one of a pregnant Mary from the 15th century – that have drawn female pilgrims seeking help for a safe and healthy pregnancy. A particular pilgrimage takes place on Pentecost Sunday, when pilgrims take it in turns to carry a 50kg candle up the hill to the church. It is said that if the candle is dropped, misfortune, war and destitution will surely follow. Legend has it that the candle fell and broke in both 1913 and 1938.

The remains of giant candles from past years carried up to St Maria Church in Bogen

Continue out of Bogen on Deggendorfer Strasse, bearing L on service road alongside main road with Bogenberg rising L. Where this ends, continue ahead on cycle track L of road. Pass **Hofweinzier** (14km, 324m) and continue under road bridge past large poultry processing factory L. Continue for 3km to **Pfelling** (17km, 315m) (accommodation, refreshments).

Turn R under main road and L past church R. Dogleg R and L to continue through village. Cross small stream and turn R to follow quiet road alongside Danube. Pass between Lenzing farm L and small chapel on riverbank and fork R on cycle track alongside flood dyke. Follow this to reach **Mariaposching** (25.5km, 315m) (accommodation, refreshments).

Pass ferry ramp and continue alongside river, eventually climbing onto flood dyke past **Kleinschwarzach** (30.5km, 314m) (camping).

Drop down onto cycle track beside flood dyke, pass under motorway bridge and continue past **Metten** L (34km, 315m) (accommodation, refreshments).

Metten (pop. 4400) is the location of Kloster St Michael, an important Benedictine abbey. Founded in AD766, it came to prominence when Charlemagne, while staying in Regensburg from 788 to 791, made it a royal abbey. After the end of the Carolingian dynasty it became a self-governing

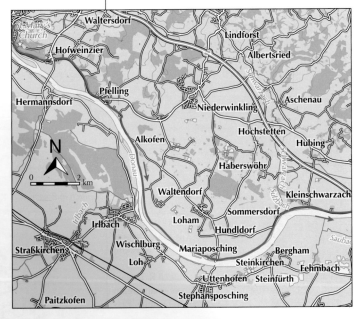

imperial abbey within the Holy Roman Empire. Members of the abbey were very active in education, both as schoolmasters and as university professors in Munich and Salzburg. After dissolution in 1803 the abbey's properties were confiscated and sold. In 1830, King Ludwig I was persuaded to allow re-establishment as well as the foundation of

Kloster St Michael Benedictine abbey in Metten houses a secondary school

a *gymnasium* (secondary school) within the abbey, which the abbey still runs. St Michael's can be visited on guided tours that include viewings of the library (which has over 150,000 books, some dating back to before the invention of the printing press), and the twin-towered abbey church.

Cross bridge over Mettenbach stream and turn L alongside stream under road bridge. Turn sharply R, then L and R onto Mettener Strasse parallel with main road R. Continue into beginning of Deggendorf.

Pass under railway line and turn immediately R (St-Florian-Weg) beside railway. Continue past fire station L and fork L on cycle track passing behind fire station, parallel with main road. Pass under two road bridges (motorway junction above), cross stream and continue to reach junction with Hans-Krämer-Strasse close to centre of **Deggendorf** (39km, 312m) (accommodation, refreshments, camping, tourist office, cycle shop, station).

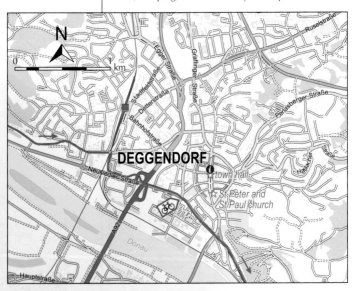

The medieval town of **Deggendorf** (pop. 32,000) grew up close to the confluence of the Danube and the Isar, a tributary that, having risen in the Austrian Tyrol, flows down through Munich on its way to the Danube. The town gained a place in infamy due to an anti-semitic pogrom in 1337, when the entire Jewish community was destroyed by fire. In 1360 a church (St Peter and St Paul) was built in the old Jewish quarter to house a monstrance containing a communion wafer said to have been miraculously saved from desecration by the Jews. For many centuries until 1968 this church was the site of the *Gnad*, an annual Catholic pilgrimage that glorified in the death of Deggendorf's Jewish population. Finally, in 1992, the Bishop of Regensburg issued a decree repudiating the wafer legend and banning its commemoration. A plaque to this effect is displayed on the church. Its closeness to the wooded hills and mountains along the German–Czech border has earned Deggendorf the soubriquet 'gateway to the Bayerischer Wald'.

Deggendorf town hall in the centre of Luitpoldplatz

STAGE 14
Deggendorf to Passau

Start	Deggendorf, Hans-Krämer-Strasse (312m)
Finish	Passau Rathausplatz (301m)
Distance	56.5km
Waymarking	Donau Radweg

The Gäuboden plain continues as far as Vilshofen, after which the rounded foothills of the Bayerischer Wald come closer to the Danube, forcing the river into a wooded gorge. The route follows the north bank, mostly close to the river, most of the way to the pretty baroque city of Passau. This stage is flat at first, then becomes gently undulating as it approaches Passau.

Leave Deggendorf heading SE on Hans-Krämer-Strasse, joining cycle track R. Continue on Hengersberger Strasse, with railway and Danube R. Bear L following road away from river into **Deggenau** (2.5km, 314m). Cross entrance to harbour and follow cycle track bearing R. Turn R and L over level crossing to follow railway L out of town. Bear L on cycle track parallel with motorway R. ◀ Just before first overbridge, turn L away from motorway, then sharply R back over bridge. Bear L on quiet road alongside flood dyke, passing **Seebach meer** L, to reach **Niederalteich** (9.5km, 314m) (accommodation, refreshments).

Between here and Niederalteich, the Isar joins the Danube on the opposite bank. Its extensive delta encompasses Isarmundung wetland bird protection sanctuary.

Niederalteich (pop. 2000) stands near the confluence of the Danube and Isar, which brings meltwater down from the Alps. As a result the area has been subject to frequent flooding. The Benedictine abbey of St Mauritius was founded in AD741 by monks who came from Reichenau abbey, on an island in Bodensee, with experience in draining swampy land for agriculture. A low spot in the abbey's history came during the Thirty Years'

map continues on page 142

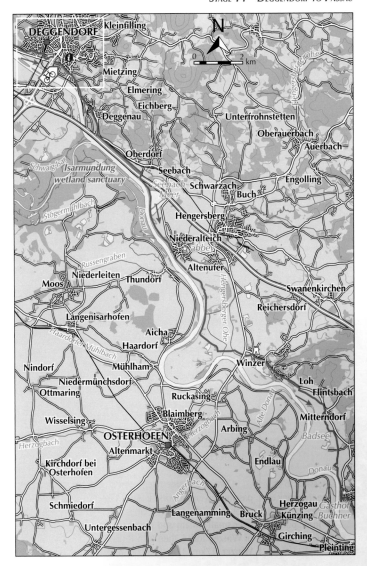

Seebach meer, near Niederalteich

War when, despite strong defensive walls, it was destroyed by Swedish troops. Reconstruction in the early 18th century produced the impressive baroque buildings seen today. There followed a period of great wealth, with the abbey drawing rent from over 170km^2 of land including vineyards in Wachau and part of the Bohemian Forest. This came to an abrupt end in 1803 with the dissolution of German monastic houses. Restoration came late and it was not until 1918 that the Benedictines returned, with abbey status being regained in 1930. Nowadays the abbey operates a school and adult education centre. It has an interest in ecumenical affairs and is unusual in having a Byzantine orthodox chapel within its cloister.

It is possible to stay on the riverbank to continue beyond Winzer, but this route is unsurfaced.

Continue beside river, soon emerging onto road and passing sewerage works L. After 4km, turn L on cycle track through fields. ◄ Turn L on country road and continue over small stream and under road bridge. At beginning of Winzer, fork L then turn R (Passauer Strasse) through **Winzer** (17km, 314m) (accommodation, refreshments).

At end of village join cycle track, R of road, continuing to **Loh**. Where cycle track ends, turn R and after 100m turn L on cycle track between fields. Bear R alongside main road to reach crossroads at beginning of **Mitterndorf** (20km, 308m).

Where cycle track ends, turn R and follow side road bearing L out of village. Continue on cycle track to reach road. Turn L, passing **Badsee** leisure lagoon behind trees R. Just before **Sattling** (21km, 306m) (refreshments), turn R on unpaved cycle track beside drainage canal and follow this through fields past **Nesslbach** (accommodation, refreshments, camping). Turn R at T-junction, then L onto riverside track. Cross a small bridge and turn R on riverside track. Drop down L beside flood dyke and continue on Donaulände into **Hofkirchen** (24km, 306m) (accommodation, refreshments, camping).

> **Hofkirchen** (pop. 3600) was an important landing station for barges plying the Danube, and a trading town with a market that was established in 1387. In 1745, the Holy Roman Emperor Francis I, husband of Maria Theresa, stayed at the Gasthof Buchner while journeying downriver on his way back to Vienna from his coronation in Frankfurt.

Gasthof Buchner in Hofkirchen is where Emperor Francis I stayed on the way home from his coronation

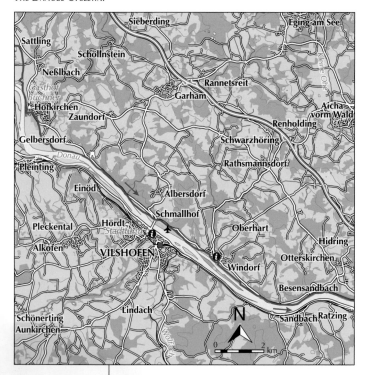

With 19th-century navigational improvements on the river, Hofkirchen lost its status as a river port. The main economic activity then became the cultivation of carding thistles for use in the woollen textile industry, although this too has now passed into history.

In middle of village turn L (Klosterstrasse), passing church L, then turn R into main road (Vishofener Strasse). Briefly join cycle track L of road, then pass sports club and turn R (sp Zum Gerwertbegebiet). Pass under power line and turn L on track between fields. Cross bridge over small stream, turn R and continue to reach Danube. Pass

Hilgartsberg L with **castle ruins** on hilltop above and continue between main road L and river R to **Schmallhof** (31.5km, 301m) (refreshments, camping). ▶

Turn R to pass under bridge, then L to pass around small airfield on cycle track beside main road. Just past airfield, bear R to continue along riverbank. Follow track back to roadside to reach beginning of Windorf. Where cycle track ends, turn immediately R beside retirement home then L along riverbank passing centre of **Windorf** (35km, 303m) (accommodation, refreshments, tourist office, cycle shop). Turn L beside side stream, then R over bridge and immediately R again to return to riverbank. Continue for 4.5km, passing ferry to Sandbach, to reach **Besensandbach** (40km, 306m).

Continue on cycle track for 2km between main road L and Danube R, then bear R along riverbank on unpaved track past **Gaishofen** (44km, 301m) (accommodation, refreshments), **Irring** (camping) and **Schalding** (46.5km, 301m) (refreshments).

Bear R along riverbank past small marina R and continue under motorway bridge. Bear L to pass under main road. Cross bridge over river Gaissa and continue

To reach Vilshofen (accommodation, refreshments, tourist office, cycle shop, station), cross bridge over Danube.

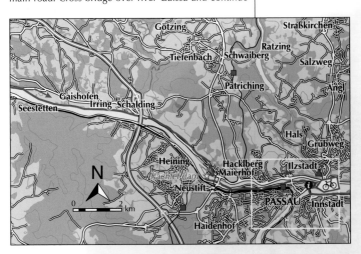

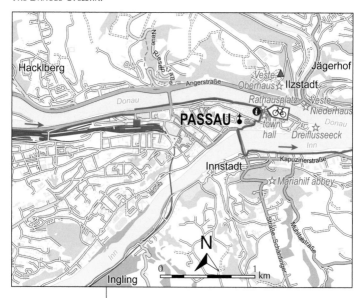

on cycle track L of road. Ascend L a short distance away from main road to pass through Donauhof, then descend through Wörth to reach **Maierhof** (51km, 308m) (refreshments).

Climb gently over another small ridge. Just before electricity sub-station R, turn sharply R and drop down to pass under main road, then continue on cycle track on opposite side of road. Turn R over **Kachlet locks and dam**, crossing Danube. Turn L along opposite bank of river and follow cycle track along riverbank.

Pass under railway and road bridges and where track reaches riverside road, turn R away from river across main road. Turn L on cycle lane R of main road. Continue between main road (Regensburger Strasse) L and railway R, bearing R to pass under road bridge. Continue over next side road. ◀

To reach Passau station, turn R on Bahnhofstrasse.

Drop down and follow cycle track bearing L under Regensburger Strasse. Cycle track continues beneath a flyover, with car park R, along riverbank. Pass under

Schanzlbrücke and continue alongside promenade past cruise boat landing quays to reach Rathausplatz in centre of **Passau** (56.5km, 301m) (accommodation, refreshments, YH, camping, tourist office, cycle shop, station).

Passau cathedral, seen from across the river Inn

The **river Inn**, at 517km long, is the greatest upper Danube tributary both in length and volume of water. Rising in the high Swiss Alps south-west of St Moritz, it flows down through the Engadine valley into Austria. Here it becomes the main river of the Tyrol, flowing right across the state through Inntal, a dramatic glacial valley between the High Alp and Northern Prealp ranges. Turning north and away from the mountains into Germany, it reaches the Danube at Passau – where its contribution of water doubles the Danube's flow. As much of this water originates in the High Alps, some from glacial meltwaters, it has a characteristic milky colour caused by dissolved limestone. This can be seen to great effect at the point where the rivers join, with the two streams of water running parallel for some distance before intermingling.

145

PASSAU

Passau (pop. 51,000) is dramatically positioned on a peninsula between the Danube and Inn rivers. As the river Ilz joins from the north at the same point, Passau is known as *Dreiflüssstadt* (three-river city) and the point at the tip of the peninsula where the rivers join as *Dreiflüsseeck* (three-river corner). Originally a Celtic settlement, the Romans set up a colony on the south side of the Inn. When they left in the fifth century, an abbey was established. From 1161 until 1803, Passau was an independent self-governing city within the Holy Roman Empire, ruled by a prince-bishop. With secularisation in 1803, the city became part of Bavaria.

Much of the city's architecture is in baroque style – the result of rebuilding following a devastating fire in 1662 that destroyed most of the altstadt. This is particularly evident in the cathedral, where a baroque nave was added to the remains of the Gothic choir and transept, creating the largest baroque church north of the Alps. The organ, with five different manuals and nearly 18,000 pipes all played from one console, is the biggest in Europe. Organ concerts are held daily in summer. North of the Danube, the Veste Oberhaus, formerly the bishops' fortress and nowadays a youth hostel, stands on a bluff overlooking the mouth of the Ilz. Passau is the starting point for many cruise boats plying the Danube, mostly going downstream as far as Budapest, but some going on to the Black Sea.

STAGE 15
Passau to Aschach

Start	Passau Rathausplatz (301m)
Finish	Aschach bridge (264m)
Distance	65km
Waymarking	Donauradweg R1 (from Austrian border)

The Danube leaves Germany and enters Austria through a narrow wooded gorge between the Bayerischer Wald and Sauwald. At Schlögen, the river's path is blocked by a hard granite ridge, forcing it to make a series of tight loops. This route starts on the right (southern) bank of the river, crosses to the left bank to avoid a section along a main road, and then crosses back after Schlögen. Villages are few and far between, but there are a series of welcoming riverside inns. A number of ruined castles stand on the hillsides above the gorge. There are waymarked routes on both banks.

Leave **Rathausplatz** in centre of Passau by following Schrottgasse uphill with Altes Rathaus L. At end turn R into cobbled Residenzplatz and immediately L (Innsbrückgasse) to pass behind Neue Residenz building. map continues on page 148

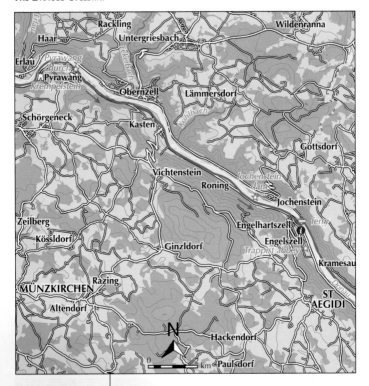

map continues
on page 151

Pass through archway into Gottfried-Schäffer-Strasse and turn L over Marienbrücke bridge crossing the Inn into **Innstadt** (refreshments). Turn L (Löwengrube) and immediately L again down steps with side ramp for pushing cycles. Turn R on cycle track beside Inn following disused railway L. Continue on Kapuzinerstrasse then dogleg L and R over level crossing into Rosenauer Weg. Continue past allotments R then bear L on narrow track beside railway (do not cross railway) to reach main road. Turn R across road and L onto cycle track beside main road (Wiener Strasse). Continue under railwaybridge and cross **German–Austrian border** (4km, 306m).

After border switch to L of road, then after 1km recross road and follow cycle track beside woodland into **Parz** (accommodation, refreshments). Continue between woods and fields to rejoin road at **Faberhof** (accommodation, refreshments). Cycle track follows R of road to Höllmühle where it passes through small **covered bridge** then changes to L to run between road and river. Pass **Burg Krempelstein** toll castle above R, then drop downhill and follow cycle track crossing to R to run between fields.

Rejoin main road at Wörth and continue to **Pyrawang** (13.5km, 291m) (accommodation, refreshments, camping). ▶ Pass through village. Soon after, cycle track crosses to L and continues past Obernzell ferry, then campsite and marina L, to reach **Kasten** (18km, 291m) (accommodation, refreshments, camping).

Continue beside road, then bear L following river past **Roning** (accommodation). Pass **Jochenstein dam** L (accommodation, refreshments) and a reproduction Roman milestone. Where cycle track ends, continue on R of road to reach beginning of **Engelhartszell** (25km, 283m) (accommodation, refreshments, camping, tourist office, cycle shop).

Pyrawang St Petrus church has recently discovered Gothic frescoes.

Jochenstein dam has improved navigation by controlling water flow through the Schlögener Schlinge

149

A village festival in Engelhartszell

Engelhartszell (pop. 1130) is a small community beside Engelszell abbey. Founded in 1293 as a Cistercian abbey by the bishop of Passau, it served for many years as a summer residence for the Prince Bishop rulers of the city and as a refuge for travellers on this thinly populated part of the Danube, until its closure in 1786. It reopened in 1925 as a monastic house for Trappist monks who had left German Alsace following its return to French control in 1919, becoming the only Trappist abbey in Austria. Despite strict vows of silence and prayer and an ageing and declining brotherhood (nine in 2009, down from 73 in 1939), the monks here – like Trappist monks everywhere – find time to operate a small distillery and brewery, producing herbal liqueurs and strong beers.

Apr–Oct, 1000–1700 (longer hours in peak season).

Do not enter village, rather turn L across main road to reach pedestrian and **cycle ferry**. ◀ Cross Danube to Urlaub and turn R on cycle track along opposite bank. Continue with view of Engelsell abbey across river R, passing hydro-electric power station in

Kramesau L (accommodation, refreshments) and small marina R (accommodation, refreshments), and emerge on main road at Rannamühl.

Turn R to reach **Niederranna** (31.5km, 287m) (accommodation, refreshments). Pass small church L and turn R. Follow road winding through village to regain riverbank and turn L passing under road bridge. Continue along riverside cycle track with steep wooded hillside L past **Freizell** (refreshments). Opposite **Schlögen**, fork R to continue along riverbank and soon reach **Au ferry** (40km, 276m) (accommodation, refreshments, camping). ▸

At **Schlögen** the Danube reaches a granite ridge across the route of the river that joins the Sauwald south-west of the river with the Mühlviertel (part of the Bohemian Massif) north-east of it. To pass through this barrier the river has cut the Schlögener Schlinge gorge – a series of tight S-shaped loops and steeply wooded slopes. The river once flowed strongly through this gorge, but hydro-electric dams at Jochenstein, Aschach and Ottersheim have slowed the flow and made for easier navigation.

Three ferries operate from Au: 1 to Schlögen (Apr–Oct, 1000–1700; longer in peak season); 2 directly across (Apr–Oct, 0900–1800; longer in peak season); 3 to Grafenau, 3km downstream (May–Sep, 0900–1800), which allows views of the tight gorge from the river.

map continues on page 152

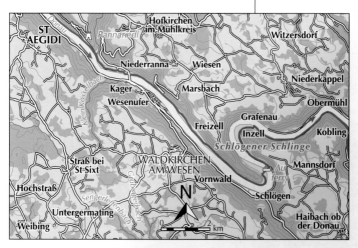

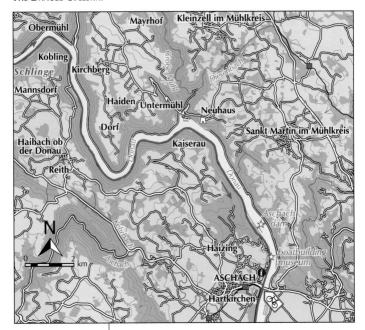

Cross Danube by ferry number 2 directly across river and turn L on quiet road following river round **Schlögener Schlinge** S-bends to reach **Inzell** (43km, 280m) (accommodation, refreshments, camping). Continue along riverbank, now on cycle track, round more bends, to **Kobling** (48km, 290m) (accommodation, refreshments).

Follow road for 600m, then fork L on cycle track round another series of bends to **Kaiserau** (58km, 281m) (accommodation, refreshments, camping). Pass Untermühl ferry ramp, with view of Schloss Neuhaus castle opposite, and continue on riverside road. Fork R to pass **Aschach dam** and hydro-electric power station. Pass **boatbuilding museum** L then turn L onto cycle track along riverbank and follow this through **Aschach** (65km, 264m) (accommodation, refreshments, tourist office, cycle shop, station).

Aschach (pop. 2200) stands below the entrance to the gorge where the Danube enters the Eferding Basin. Once a boatbuilding and shipping centre, where goods were transferred onto special barges to pass through the dangerous waters of the Schlögener Schlinge, Aschach is now a sleepy riverside town, with a few traditional old houses, a 16th-century castle and a *schopper* (traditional barge) boatbuilding museum to recall its heyday. The Aschach hydro-electric dam and power station was Europe's largest when it opened in 1964.

STAGE 16
Aschach to Linz

Start	Aschach bridge (264m)
Finish	Urfahr (Linz), Nibelungen bridge (254m)
Distance	26.5km
Waymarking	Donauradweg R1

Beyond Aschach the valley widens as the Danube enters the fertile farmlands of the Eferdinger Basin. This short stage is mostly flat, closely following the right (southern) bank of the river to Ottensheim then crossing by cable ferry to the left bank, before ending in Urfahr opposite the industrial city of Linz.

Follow cycle track beside Danube S under **Aschach bridge** and continue between Danube L and road R to reach **Brandstatt** (3km, 263m) (accommodation, refreshments). Turn sharply L on road around small harbour, then fork L on riverside cycle track to reach **Ottensheim dam** and power station. Bear R away from river to emerge on dam service road. Follow this for 750m, crossing the Innbach river and turn sharply L in hamlet of **Fall** (14.5km, 265m) (refreshments, camping).

The direct route along the south bank from Ufer to Linz follows a busy road with no cycle lanes, therefore it is better to follow the north bank route, as described here.

Turn L again onto cycle track alongside the Innbach and follow this through woodland to reach ferry landing stage in **Ufer** (refreshments). ◄ Cross Danube by chain ferry (frequent 0615–1915) to **Ottensheim** (17km, 259m) (accommodation, refreshments, camping, tourist office, station).

In 1228 **Ottensheim** (pop. 4500) was granted the right to hold a regular market, only the third community in Upper Austria to receive this privilege, and this market in the main square has continued to the present day. An attractive castle (built in 1527) stands on a small rise above the town. Privately owned, it is not open to visitors. When Ottensheim hydro-electric dam was built in the 1970s, an old arm of the river became a backwater. This has been converted into an international standard 2km rowing lake, which held the World Rowing Championships in 2008. The ungainly looking chain ferry across the

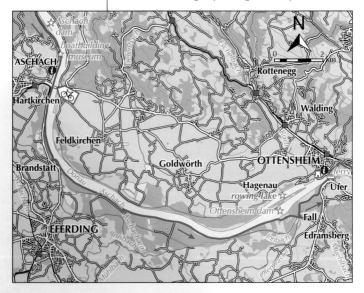

Danube, linking Ottensheim with Ufer, is driven across the river by the strength of the current.

After crossing river, turn immediately R (Siglallee) and bear L into Sportplatzstrasse. Bear L before sports club and follow cycle track over Bleicherbach stream.

The Ufer to Ottensheim ferry is propelled by the force of the current

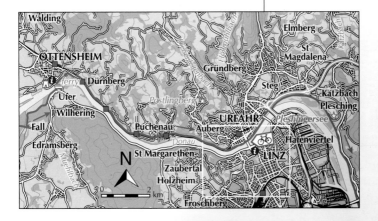

Turn R between stream R and main road L, then turn L under road and across railway. Turn R on road, passing back under main road, to reach **Dürnberg** (18.5km, 263m) (refreshments, station).

Pass restaurant and turn immediately L under main road for a third time, and continue on cycle track L of road. Follow this through **Puchenau** (22.5km, 269m) (accommodation, station) passing **station** R. Continue over crossroads and follow cycle track ahead. Emerge onto Anschlussmauer, continuing beside main road before rejoining cycle track.

At beginning of **Urfahr** (accommodation, refreshments, cycle shop, station) turn R under main road and dogleg R and L to reach riverbank. Continue along riverbank (Obere Donaustrasse) to reach **Nibelungenbrücke bridge** over Danube linking Urfahr with **Linz** (26.5km, 254m) (accommodation, refreshments, YH, tourist office, cycle shop, station). ◄

To visit Linz, turn sharply L before bridge (Flussgasse), then R (Fiedlerstrasse) and R again past new town hall. Cross Danube on Nibelungenbrücke bridge to reach Hauptplatz.

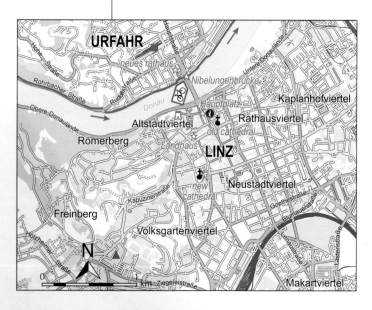

Hauptplatz, in centre of Linz, with the Holy Trinity column and lined with baroque buildings

LINZ

Linz (pop. 191,000) is the third largest city in Austria and the largest port on the middle Danube. Originally a Roman settlement, it came to prominence when Habsburg Emperor Friedrich III (1415–1493) built the castle and made Linz, albeit briefly, capital of Austria. As an important trade crossroads, particularly for salt and iron, a market grew up in an area now occupied by Hauptplatz, a huge medieval square surrounded by baroque buildings at the heart of the city. In the centre of this square is the *Dreifaltigkeitsäule* (Holy Trinity Column), which was erected in 1700 in thanksgiving of deliverance from war, fire and the plague. There are two cathedrals: the neo-Gothic Neuer Dom (south of the centre), which seats 20,000 and is the largest church in Austria, and the Jesuit Alter Dom, where the composer Anton Bruckner (1824–1896) was organist. The Landhaus, formerly a Renaissance abbey where Johannes Kepler (1571–1630) taught mathematics and promulgated his theory of planetary motion, now houses the Oberösterreich state parliament. A narrow gauge mountain tramway (Pöstlingbergbahn) links the city centre with the suburb of Pöstlingberg, on a hilltop north of Urfahr, where there are extensive views of the city and a much-visited pilgrimage church.

Adolf Hitler regarded Linz as his home and had plans to make it both cultural capital of the Third Reich and an industrial powerhouse. Industrial development was encouraged along the Danube extending south-east from the city, dominated by Austria's largest steelworks and chemical works. Culturally the city has remained prominent, hosting a number of galleries, museums and music events, including an annual Bruckner festival.

STAGE 17
Linz to Mauthausen

Start	Urfahr (Linz), Nibelungenbrücke bridge (254m)
Finish	Mauthausen, Heindlkai (241m)
Distance	24.5km
Waymarking	Donauradweg R1

This short stage starts by closely following the Danube's left bank between the hills of Mühlviertel and the extensive industrial suburbs of Linz on the opposite bank. Turning away from the river, the route passes below the remains of Mauthausen concentration camp, preserved as a memorial to victims of Nazi atrocities, before returning to the riverside at Mauthausen.

From underneath N side of **Nibelungenbrücke bridge**, connecting Urfahr with Linz, follow riverside cycle track (Heinrich-Gleissner-Promenade) NE past cruise boat landing stages. Just before railway bridge, turn L away from Danube then R under bridge. Continue under motorway bridge and follow flood dyke round a sweeping bend with low-lying meadows of Pleschinger Au R. Bear L onto dyke and pass **Pleschingersee lake** behind trees L (4.5km, 256m) (camping).

Continue along dyke with industrial area of Linz on opposite side of river R. Pass under road and rail bridges, with **steelworks** and confluence of Traun river R. Dogleg around **Rosenau marina** (12km, 251m) and continue to reach a path junction 1km before Abwinden dam. Turn L away from river and cross small bridge over flood relief channel. Turn R before main road and L through underpass. Bear R (Im Fall) climbing gently through **Abwinden** (16km, 248m) (accommodation, refreshments).

Fork R and pass St Georgen station. At beginning of **St Georgen** (accommodation, refreshments), turn R on cycle track and continue on concrete bridge over Gusen stream. This bridge was built by slave labour prisoners in 1941 to provide a rail link with Gusen concentration camp.

Turn L (Wimmingerstrasse) and R at T-junction onto main road (Mauthausener Strasse) on cycle track R. At end of St Georgen, cycle track bears briefly R away from road (Koglberg) then returns to road at beginning of **Gusen**. Bear R again away from road (Bachstrasse), rejoining main road (now Georgestrasse) at end of village. Fork L and continue through **Langenstein** (21.5km, 246m) (accommodation, refreshments) on Hauptstrasse. Drop downhill round series of bends to reach road fork. ▶

Fork R (Linzer Strasse) and climb over small ridge. After 1.25km, turn R (Josef-Czerwenka-Strasse) beside high school R and follow road bending L parallel to main road. Continue onto cycle track beside main road

The road to the left leads steeply uphill to Mauthausen concentration camp, where many original buildings remain as a gruesome but sobering memorial to victims of Nazi atrocities.

map continues on page 160

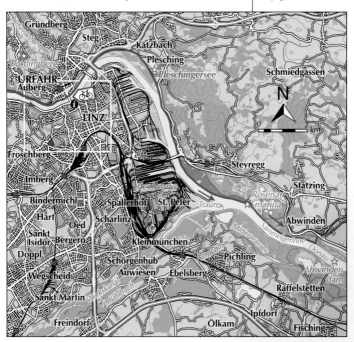

Near Gusen the route crosses a bridge built by slave labour and passes a memorial to concentration camp victims

and where this ends continue through car park and past **Schloss Pragstein castle** R to reach Heindlkai in centre of **Mauthausen** (24.5km, 241m) (accommodation, refreshments, tourist office, cycle shop, station).

Mauthausen (pop. 5000) was established in about AD1000 as a toll station (*maut* is German for 'toll') collecting revenues from passing boats. It has a

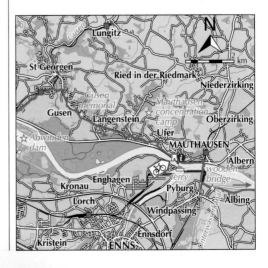

picturesque old town, 15th-century church and 16th-century castle. Unfortunately, Mauthausen's recent history is more gruesome. From 1938 to 1945 a large Nazi concentration camp operated west of the town. Initially most of the inmates were political prisoners from Austria and Germany who were used as slave labour in granite quarries, producing building materials for use in Linz and Nurnberg. Later, large numbers of prisoners arrived from other countries invaded by the Nazis, including many from Poland and prisoners of war from the Soviet Union. The most infamous of punishments was for prisoners to carry heavy granite blocks up 186 steps from the camp quarry, a route that became known as 'the stairway of death'. Approximately 100,000 prisoners died here.

Prisoner's mural at Mauthausen concentration camp showing 'stairway of death'

STAGE 18
Mauthausen to Grein

Start	Mauthausen, Heindlkai (241m)
Finish	Grein ferry ramp (240m)
Distance	39km
Waymarking	Donauradweg EV6

During this stage, the route travels south of the Danube, using quiet country roads away from the river, and leading between gently rolling hills and the fertile agricultural land of the Mostviertel (cider quarter). After Ardagger–Markt, wooded hills close in again as the riverside is followed to Grein. The going is mostly flat.

Pyburg log bridge over the Oberwasserkanal is claimed to be Europe's longest

Alternative route avoiding Mauthausen bridge

Mauthausen bridge can be a busy road. A quieter alternative can be found by taking the **ferry** from Mauthausen to **Pyburg** (May–Sep, 0900–1800), continuing E to pass under bridge, then taking first turn on R to rejoin main route on quiet road on S side of bridge.

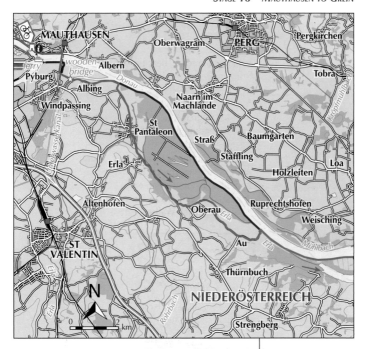

For the main route, from Heindlkai, in centre of Mauthausen, cycle E through car park. Dogleg R and L across main road onto cycle track beside Danube. Just before Mauthausen bridge, turn L and follow road curving R onto bridge and cross Danube. After bridge, turn L under railway. ▶ Follow quiet road ahead to reach a **wooden bridge** over **Oberwasserkanal**.

Cross bridge and turn L alongside canal and continue past Albing R (3.5km, 240m). Continue to reach Danube and fork L onto flood dyke. After 600m drop down R off flood dyke.

Alternative route via flood dyke

By continuing ahead along flood dyke, you can cycle directly towards **Wallsee-Mittelkirchen dam**, saving

map continues
on page 164

Alternative route avoiding Mauthausen bridge rejoins main route here.

2km. Mostly asphalt, but includes 2km of rough unsurfaced track.

For the main route, bear L and turn immediately R away from river, continuing on quiet road between fields to enter **St Pantaleon** (7km, 241m) (accommodation, refreshments) on Steinerstrasse.

Pass church R and fork L (Erlastrasse). Pass through **Erla**, ascending gently, and continue, winding through trees and fields. Fork L into **Oberau**, then turn L at T-junction. Turn L again at next T-junction to pass through **Au**. After passing church, follow road bearing L. Continue up and over flood dyke, cross flood relief channel and emerge on riverbank. ◄ Turn R alongside Danube and continue to reach **Wallsee-Mittelkirchen dam**.

Alternative route via flood dyke rejoins main route here.

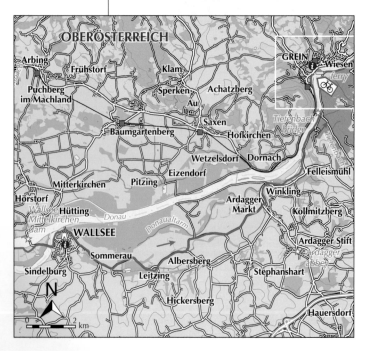

Just before dam, turn R away from river and fork L to circle round power station. Emerge into large car park and turn R on dam approach road. Cross bridge over old arm of Danube and turn L on riverside road, with **Wallsee** (21km, 233m) (accommodation, refreshments, tourist office) on hillside R.

> **Wallsee** (pop. 2100) was the site of a fifth-century Roman camp built for 1000 soldiers on the sandstone outcrop overlooking a bend in the Danube to protect their borders from Germanic tribes living north of the river. In 1368, 900 years later, the same site was used for a castle built by a local ruler. In 1859 the castle was purchased by a daughter of Austrian Emperor Archduke Franz Joseph, and it has remained in family hands ever since. For many centuries, until 1895, Wallsee's sandstone rock was used to produce millstones, which were shipped downriver to equip flour mills throughout the Austro-Hungarian Empire.

Continue on Uferstrasse along riverbank, passing below castle R. This road circles town and emerges on road from Wallsee to Sommerau. Turn L and continue on cycle track (at first L of road but soon crossing to R) to reach hamlet of **Sommerau** (refreshments, camping). Continue beside road, winding through fields. Shortly before next village, follow cycle track bearing R over small bridge to reach **Leitzing** (26km, 229m) (accommodation, refreshments).

Turn L and R by Gasthof Parlament, a *birnmosthaus* (perry and cider house), with giant wooden pear in garden, to rejoin road and continue on cycle track beside road. After 1.5km, turn L and continue on roadside cycle track. Cross main road and turn L at T-junction into **Ardagger-Markt** (32km, 235m) (accommodation, refreshments, camping).

> **Ardagger-Markt** (pop. 1000), located beside the Zeitbach off an old arm of the Danube, is a sleepy

A giant wooden pear outside a perry and cider house at Leitzing, in the Mostviertel (cider quarter)

village with a farming museum. Ardagger Stift abbey, 2.5km south of the main village, has a church where the St Margaret windows are made with the oldest stained glass in Austria (1240). Outside the abbey is the Mostbirnhaus, where you can sample *birnmost* (perry made from locally grown pears) and *most* (apple cider).

Continue through town to reach main road. Cross road and turn R on track, eventually forking L through trees with old arm of Danube L. Pass **Felleismühl** R (on other side of main road) and continue to emerge on main road by extensive quarries. Follow cycle tack L of road, with Danube L, to reach **Tiefenbach bridge** (accommodation, refreshments). Pass under bridge and turn immediately R on cycle track curving up onto bridge. Cross Danube (cycle lane R) and turn R on main road. At bottom of bridge approach, turn sharply back R and after 50m turn L along riverside cycle track.

Follow this past Ufer, bearing L to pass marina R. Cross small stream and pass campsite L. Continue along riverbank to reach ferry ramp of **ferry** to Weisen in **Grein**

(39km, 240m) (accommodation, refreshments, camping, tourist office, cycle shop).

The attractive small town of **Grein** (pop. 3100) developed during medieval times, its importance coming from being positioned at the entrance to the Strudengau gorge. Here barges were unloaded to transport cargoes past the rapids and this attracted merchants, traders and river pilots. The wealth this generated helped found the oldest unmodernised popular theatre in Austria (1791), when an old grain silo was converted into a theatre. It has many unique elements, including lockable seats for the wealthy, a prison cell with viewing slits for prisoners and a toilet shielded only by a curtain. The castle overlooking the town centre, the oldest residential palace in Austria, now houses the Upper Austrian maritime museum, which traces the history of shipping on the Danube and its tributaries.

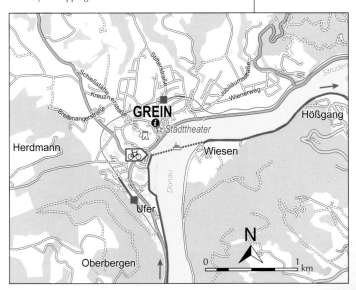

STAGE 19
Grein to Melk

Start	Grein ferry ramp (240m)
Finish	Melk, Kremser Strasse (209m)
Distance	47km
Waymarking	Donauradweg EV6

Immediately after Grein, the Danube cuts through the hard granite of the Waldviertel (wooded quarter) by way of the narrow Strudengau gorge. Rocky cliffs line the valley, often topped with ruined castles. Beyond Ybbs, the valley opens into the wide agricultural Nibelungengau plain before ending below the stunning baroque abbey of Melk. This completely flat route closely follows the right (southern) bank throughout, mostly on quiet riverside roads, towpaths or flood dykes.

From **ferry ramp** in Grein, take ferry (May–Sep, 0900–1800) across Danube to **Wiesen**. Turn L and follow riverside road passing below **Hössgang** (accommodation, refreshments) on hillside R. Continue on road and after

Grein and Wiesen are connected by a cycle ferry

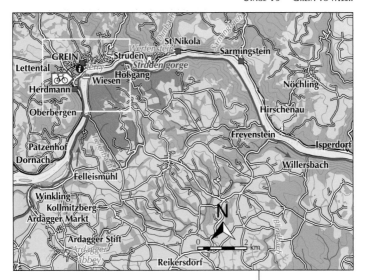

700m fork L beside river with view of first Struden then St Nikola, both on opposite bank.

map continues
on page 170

> For medieval riverfarers, the **Struden gorge** was the most treacherous stretch of the Danube. Forced between narrow granite cliffs of the Waldviertel, the river rushed through a gorge filled with hidden rocks and whirlpools. This obstacle was reduced when Hössgang canal was dug in order to bypass the gorge's narrowest part, creating Wörth Island, and it was finally eliminated by the series of post-Second World War hydro-electric dams built to control the flow and level of the river. Schloss Werfenstein castle overlooks the narrows.

Follow cycle track through the gorge between wooded hillside R and Danube L for 6.5km to **Freyenstein** (9.5km, 229m) (accommodation, refreshments). Continue along riverbank, now on a quiet road, to **Willersbach** (12km, 230m) (accommodation, refreshments, camping).

169

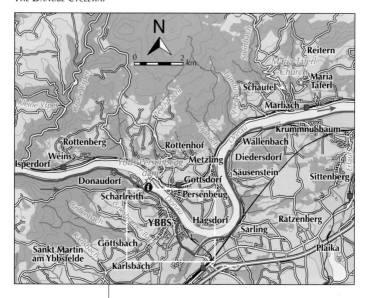

map continues
on page 172

Soon reach **Donaudorf** (17.5km, 230m) (refreshments) and **Scharlreith** (18.5km, 227m) (accommodation, refreshments, tourist office) beside **Ybbs-Persenbeug dam**. Bear R onto main road (cycle track L), passing Ybbs tourist information office L, then fork L on cycle track into woods.

Turn R (Donaulände) alongside river to reach boat landing stage in centre of **Ybbs** (20.5km, 217m) (accommodation, refreshments, station).

Ybbs (pop. 5500) has an attractively preserved medieval old centre right beside the Danube. The course of Stadtgraben (the old city moat) and fortifications can be traced looping round the ancient centre. In the old town is a cycle museum that has many historic machines on display, including penny-farthings.

Continue past Passauerkasten and on through riverside gardens. Pass **Pulverturm tower** R and follow road, turning R. At crossroads, take cycle track diagonally opposite L (beside a small shrine), passing allotments. Cross side road and continue into Wüsterstrasse then go ahead at roundabout into **Bahnhofstrasse** (cycle track L of road). Drop down through underpass, then cross bridge over **Ybbs river**. After bridge turn immediately L along riverbank. Pass under railway bridge and continue on cycle track through wetland nature reserve to reach **Sarling** (accommodation). Turn L and R beside Danube and continue through village on Unterhaus Strasse. At end of village continue on cycle track between railway R and river L to reach **Säusenstein** (27km, 217m) (accommodation, station).

Continue along riverbank to **Diedersdorf**, where you turn R away from river and L through village on road beside railway. At end of village, turn L to rejoin riverbank. At **Wallenbach**, turn R away from river and L to join road. Continue on road past small harbour L into **Krummnussbaum** (31.5km, 213m) (accommodation, refreshments, station).

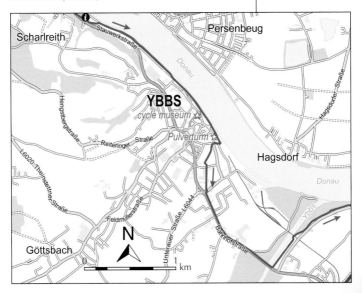

Turn L just before Gasthaus Schiffmeister, then bear R over flood dyke to reach riverside track. Pass Marbach ferry, with Maria Taferl pilgrimage church clearly visible on hilltop opposite. Continue beside Danube for 3.5km to reach **river Erlauf**.

Turn R beside Erlauf, then bear R onto flood dyke and turn L over bridge. Turn L along flood dyke on opposite bank to return to Danube, then R along riverbank past **Pöchlarn** (36.5km, 213m) (accommodation, refreshments, station).

Pöchlarn (pop. 4000) is a small town that featured in the historic German *Nibelungenlied* folk saga. While the centrepiece of this story is the court at Worms, and most of the action takes place on the Rhine, cities as varied as Verona (Italy), Esztergom (Hungary) and Pöchlarn also had roles. A monument between the town and the Danube promenade celebrates this by displaying the coats of arms

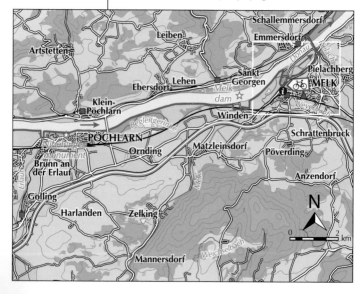

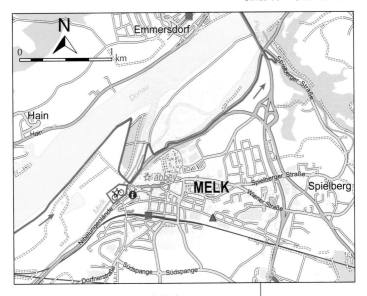

of 16 towns mentioned. More recently, Pöchlarn was the birthplace and home of the artist Oskar Kokoschka (1886–1980). His birthplace can be visited. The old Welserturm tower, built as a defence tower and then used for many years as a salt warehouse, now houses the city museum.

After Pöchlarn pass large modern mill R, then pass under road bridge and continue beside river for 6km to reach Melk dam. Turn R at dam entrance, pass under railway and follow track bearing L to reach T-junction. Turn L again, back under railway and immediately R beside railway. Turn L to follow track back to Danube and R alongside river to reach Melk campsite.

Turn sharply R (Kolomaniau) continuing into Rollfährestrasse and cross St Leopoldbrücke bridge over Melk river to reach **Melk** (47km, 209m) (accommodation, refreshments, YH, camping, tourist office, station).

The library of Stift Melk Benedictine abbey has a highly frescoed ceiling and a collection of medieval manuscripts

MELK

For some kilometres as you cycle towards Melk (pop. 5250) the view ahead is dominated by Stift Melk Benedictine abbey, boldly standing on a rocky bluff 50m above the town. This site is important not only for the monastic buildings, regarded as the epitome of baroque in Austria, but also because they represent the cradle of the Austrian nation. The Babenberg princely family from Bavaria moved to Melk in AD976 and made it capital of the Oestermarch (the eastern borderland of the Holy Roman Empire and an area intended to be a border state between Bavaria and Hungary). By 1156, when the capital moved to Vienna, the area under Babenberg control had grown into the Oesterreich (eastern empire). In 1089 the Babenberg Margrave Leopold II gave his castle at Melk to the Benedictines, who used it as the base for a new abbey.

The current baroque edifice was constructed by Jakob Prandtauer between 1702 and 1736. Of particular note are the highly frescoed abbey church and the library, which has a priceless collection of medieval manuscripts. The Imperial quarters were built to accommodate the emperor, who would stop overnight with his huge retinue when travelling to visit the western parts of his empire. Melk abbey's fame and academic status enabled it to survive the vicissitudes of the Napoleonic Wars, when monastic institutions throughout Europe were dissolved. During the Anschluss (1938), its property was confiscated by the state, but it was returned after the Second World War. Nowadays, in addition to being a major tourist attraction, the abbey houses a school for 900 pupils.

Huddled below the abbey, the old town centre of Melk has a large number of interesting buildings from a wide period of history but, as this is a must-stop destination for Danube cruise boats, it can become very crowded with tourists.

STAGE 20
Melk to Krems

Start	Melk, Kremser Strasse (209m)
Finish	Krems, Bahnhofplatz (200m)
Distance	37.5km
Waymarking	Donauradweg EV6

The attractive stretch of river between Melk and Krems, known as the Wachau, is extensively planted with orchards and vineyards and produces some of Austria's finest wines. The route follows the Danube's left bank, sometimes through vineyards and sometimes on the riverbank, passing through a series of wine-producing villages. The wooded hills of Waldviertel rise behind the vineyards.

From corner of Kremser Strasse and Nibelungenlände in **Melk**, follow **Nibelungenlände** NE on cycle track between road R and **River Melk** L, with **Stift Melk abbey** towering above R. After 200m, fork L on cycle track parallel with river. Just before cruise boat ticket office, turn sharply R (Pionierstrasse) and turn L at T-junction on cycle track L of road. Where road forks, cross road junction and follow cycle track beside L fork (cycle track on R of road). Continue on road, go under bridge, then turn

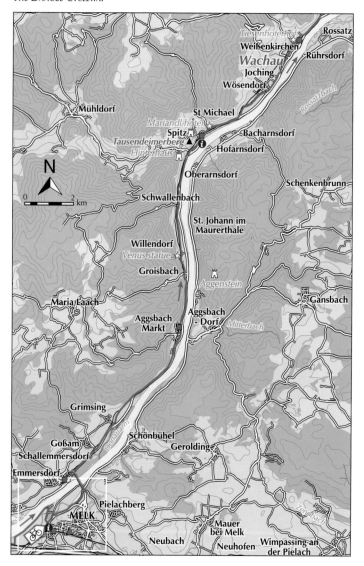

immediately R and R again to climb steeply onto bridge and cross Danube. Curve round L after bridge to reach roundabout on outskirts of **Emmersdorf** (4km, 215m) (accommodation, refreshments, camping, station).

map continues
on page 179

Turn L at roundabout on cycle track beside main road. After 1km, cross road and pass through **Schallemmersdorf** on service road. Dogleg R and L over stream and continue out of village beside main road. Continue beside main road and after 1km fork L on cycle track, passing **Grimsing** L (station). Follow cycle track through fields back to road and continue beside it through narrow valley with railway L and Danube R. Fork L, to cycle through **Aggsbach Markt** (11km, 209m) (accommodation, refreshments, station).

Go straight ahead through village, then rejoin main road and continue on cycle track with view of Schloss Aggenstein castle on hilltop opposite. Fork L through **Groisbach** (13.5km, 219m) (accommodation) and continue beside railway through **Willendorf** (14.5km, 219m) (accommodation, refreshments, station).

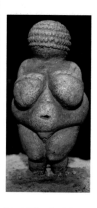

The **Willendorf Venus**, an 11cm limestone effigy of a plump female figure, was discovered in 1908 during excavations for a new railway line. It is believed to be a Palaeolithic female fertility symbol, the most realistic object from this period discovered in Europe. The original is in a museum in Vienna, but an oversized version stands on the site where it was discovered and there is a copy in a small museum close to the cycleway.

The Willendorf Venus

Follow cycle track through apricot orchards to **Schwallenbach** (16.5km, 212m) (accommodation, refreshments, station). Continue through vineyards as valley narrows again. Pass quarry L and closely follow railway and road through gorge. Bear L away from main road into **Spitz** (19km, 206m) (accommodation, refreshments, tourist office, station).

Tausendeimerberg vineyard in Spitz is said to produce 1000 buckets of wine in a good year

The *Tausendeimerberg* (thousand-bucket hill), so called because in a good year it can produce 1000 buckets (56,000 litres) of wine, rises directly behind **Spitz** (pop. 1700). The well-preserved 13th-century Hinterhaus ruined castle stands on a rocky outcrop west of the village, while the Rotes Tor gateway, the scene of a bloody battle during the Thirty Years' War, is located among vineyards to the north. At the exit to the village is the Mariandl hotel, the setting for a series of popular Austrian films in the early 1960s about a girl living in a hotel who aspires to a musical scholarship. English versions of the theme song *Mariandl* were recorded by Petula Clark and Jimmy Young. The Gunter Phillip Museum at the hotel is dedicated to one of the stars of the films.

Bear R (Mittergasse) and follow this bearing L into Rollfährestrasse under railway bridge. Turn R parallel with railway (Bahnhofstrasse), passing station R and continue ahead into Kremser Strasse to leave village passing **Mariandl hotel** L. Cross railway and bear L onto cycle track between railway and main road. Bear L away from road into **St Michael** (21.5km, 215m) (accommodation, refreshments). ▸ Bear L in village (Hauptstrasse) and follow this winding through vineyards to reach **Wösendorf** (23km, 207m) (accommodation, refreshments). Turn R by church (still Hauptstrasse) and L to run parallel with main road. Continue through **Joching** (24km, 202m) (accommodation, station) on Josef-Jarnek-Strasse (named after a local wine pioneer). After village this becomes Landstrasse, leading into centre of **Weissenkirchen** (25km, 207m) (accommodation, refreshments, tourist office, station).

At St Michael the route enters the Wachau proper and from here to beyond Weissenkirchen vineyards run uninterrupted for 7km along the valley side.

> **Weissenkirchen** (pop. 1500) is the principal wine village of the Wachau. This picturesque village has frescoed and decorated courtyards, narrow lanes and a partly fortified 14th-century white church. Weissenkirchen is said to be the original home of the Riesling grape, a theory that can be checked out in the local wine museum, formerly a 17th-century salt warehouse, or in the Tiesenhoferhof, an arcaded 15th-century Renaissance building that houses the Austrian Wine Academy.

Bear L over railway level crossing, then R (still Landstrasse). Turn L (Untere Bachgasse) then R into Marktplatz. Continue ahead into Kremser Strasse out of

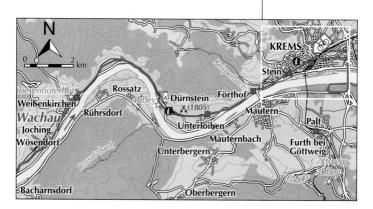

town and bear R over another level crossing to rejoin main road. Follow cycle track between road and railway with vineyards climbing up valley side L. Bear L, following railway away from river and cycle through vineyards, before returning to riverside. Continue beside road around long sweeping river bend. Pass statue of Richard Lionheart and Blondel L, with view of ruined Schloss Kuenringer castle ahead, and bear L (Hauptstrasse), uphill into **Dürnstein** (30.5km, 221m) (accommodation, refreshments, tourist office, station).

Continue through centre of town, pass through Stadttor city gate and bear R through underpass to cross main road. Pass station L and continue through vineyards, passing Franzosendenkmal L. ◀ Where road turns R, continue ahead on quiet road ascending through vineyards with railway L. Pass **Unterloiben station** L (32.5km, 214m) (accommodation, refreshments, station) and

This large monument commemorates the Napoleonic War Battle of Dürnstein (1805) between a French division and a combined Austro-Russian force.

DÜRNSTEIN

Dürnstein (pop. 900) is a village that boasts a fame and attractiveness to tourists that far exceeds its small size. Above the town stand the ruins of Kuenringer castle, where the English King Richard the Lionheart was held prisoner for three months in 1193. During the Third Crusade, Richard had offended Leopold V, Duke of Austria, who found the opportunity to take his revenge by imprisoning Richard as he made his way back from Palestine via central Europe. He was eventually released after payment of a huge ransom, money that went towards setting up the new Austrian city of Wiener Neustadt and which also paid for the strengthening of the walls at Hainburg. The legend that Richard's personal troubadour, Blondel, travelled around European castles seeking his master by singing a song only they knew outside the windows has no credence, as Leopold made no secret that he was holding Richard at Dürnstein. The castle survived until 1645, when it was destroyed by Swedish forces during the Thirty Years' War.

In the middle of the village is Stift Dürnstein Augustinian abbey. Founded in 1410, the baroque structure standing today was built between 1710 and 1740. The monastic order was dissolved in 1788, less than 50 years after completion of the building. The stunning blue painted tower was restored in 1986.

*Steiner Tor gateway
in Krems replete with
fairy tale features*

descend to reach road junction. Bear L beside road and
very soon join cycle track beside main road. Continue
through **Förthof** on Förthofstrasse, passing approach road
to Mauternerbrücke bridge R. At beginning of Stein turn
R across main road (do not continue under archway into
Stein) and L on cycle track beside Steiner Donaulände.

Pass **Stein** L (36.5km, 198m) (accommodation,
refreshments, cycle shop, station) and continue ahead
at roundabout into Ringstrasse (cycle track R). ▶ Go
under railway bridge, passing youth hostel R, into **Krems**
(37.5km, 200m) (accommodation, refreshments, YH,

Stein and Krems
are one continuous
built-up area.

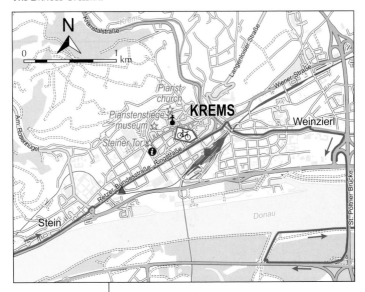

camping, tourist office, cycle shop, station). This stage ends at intersection of Ringstrasse and Bahnhofplatz, with station 100m R.

Krems (pop. 24,000) is a modern industrial town with a medieval old town at its heart. The main landmark, the Steiner Tor gateway, has a baroque tower with two side towers that have steeply sloping spires, making them look like fairy tale pixie houses. The highly baroqued St Viet parish church stands among a maze of medieval streets. Slightly above it, on the slopes of Wachtberg, is the Piaristenkirche, the most attractive of Krems' many churches. Piaristenstiege, a narrow covered stairway between houses, connects the two churches. The church of the old Dominican abbey now houses a wine museum.

STAGE 21
Krems to Tulln

Start	Krems, Bahnhofplatz (200m)
Finish	Tulln, Nibelungen monument (175m)
Distance	44.5km
Waymarking	Donauradweg EV6

Leaving the Wachau, the Danube enters the flat Tullnerfeld plain. This route crosses the river at Krems and follows a quiet, good-quality riverside trail most of the way to Tulln. This area is the energy powerhouse of Austria, with hydro-electric, nuclear and thermal power stations passed en route.

From the junction with Bahnhofplatz, 100m N of **Krems station**, head NE on Wachaustrasse (cycle track R). Cross bridge over **Krems river** and turn next R (Hohensteinstrasse). Pass under railway bridge and bear R onto cycle track. Bear R, dropping down to cycle beside river. Pass under two bridges and just before third bridge climb back L onto flood dyke. Turn R across river and L

map continues on page 184

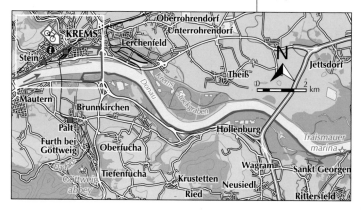

along other bank (Rechte Kremszelle). Pass police station R and immediately before motorway overbridge, turn R on cycle track beside motorway slip road. Turn L under slip road, then L again curving up and onto motorway bridge and cross Danube on cycle track beside road with Göttweig abbey visible on hilltop ahead.

Beyond bridge follow cycle track bearing R beside slip road. After 700m turn R away from road and zig-zag L and R onto cycle track beside drainage canal. Follow this to reach Danube and bear R along riverbank. Pass under motorway bridge, then dogleg away from river around small marina. Continue beside Danube for 11km, passing **Hollenburg** R (accommodation, refreshments) and going under another motorway bridge to reach **Traismauer marina** (17km, 187m) (refreshments, camping).

Pass between marina L and restaurant R to continue along riverbank for another 7km. Shortly before **Altenwörth dam** (24km, 186m), turn R away from river through woods. Bear L through trees parallel with **Traisen river** R to reach dam service road. Turrn R over Traisen then L to drop down to other side of river and continue beside river to reach Danube. Follow Danube riverside cycle track for 1.5km and, where this ends, turn R away from river on cycle track winding through woods. Cross a backwater and emerge into large open area surrounding

map continues
on page 186

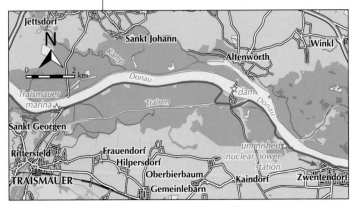

184

The abandoned Zwentendorf nuclear power station

the buildings of an unfinished **nuclear power station** (refreshments). ▶

Turn L to pass between river and planned reactor building and leave compound through its main gate. Turn immediately L to regain riverbank and continue past **Zwentendorf** (31km, 179m) (accommodation, refreshments, camping).

Fork L to continue along riverbank without entering the village. Turn R away from river into woods, then after 150m turn L at entrance to **Erpersdorf** continuing through woodland. Pass between trees L and small village of **Klein-Schönbichl**. Pass marina L and continue beside Danube for 250m. Bear R alongside Perschling river. Emerge onto main road and turn L (cycle track L of road) across Perschling. Pass under overhead conveyor and cross series of industrial railway lines serving chemical works. Opposite main entrance to works, turn R across road towards **Pischelsdorf** (34.5km, 181m) (accommodation, refreshments).

Just before first houses, turn L on cycle track skirting village R. Fork L and after 100m, turn L before woods. Just before reaching main road, turn R over small stream.

Zwentendorf was planned to be Austria's first nuclear power station. Work ceased in 1979 after a referendum voted against nuclear power.

Tulln motorway bridge

Turn immediately L under main road and follow cycle track curving round R to run beside road. Bear L away from road under power lines and follow quiet country lane winding beside fields to reach **Langenschönbichl** (37.5km, 180m) (accommodation, refreshments). Continue through village (Hauptstrasse) and by last

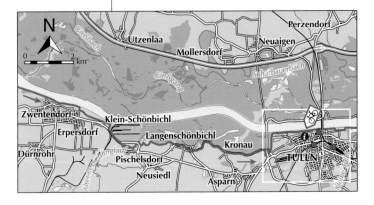

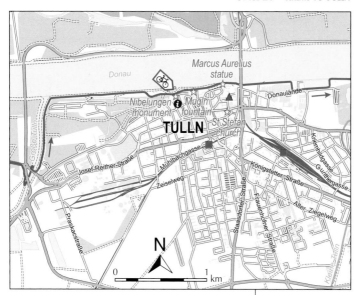

houses turn L (Ziegelofenstrasse). Follow this road, winding between fields R and marshy Danube backwaters L to reach **Kronau** (accommodation, refreshments).

Continue past village and after 1.5km, turn R on cycle track just before roundabout. Follow this to reach banks of **Grosse Tulln river** and turn sharply L along flood dyke. Pass under two road bridges and after second bridge turn sharply back L up onto road and turn L across river. Immediately after bridge, turn L alongside Grosse Tulln. Bear L (R track is for pedestrians) and follow cycle track below flood dyke to reach Danube. Bear R, and climb onto flood dyke then continue past small harbour L to reach **Nibelungen monument** R close to the centre of **Tulln** (44.5km, 175m) (accommodation, refreshments, YH, camping, tourist office, cycle shop, station).

187

TULLN

Tulln (pop. 15,000) was the site of a Roman cavalry camp called Comagena and a well-preserved horseshoe-shaped Roman tower survives from this period. In the early days of Austria, the town was briefly (1089–1156) the capital of Babenberg Oesterreich (the forerunner of modern Austria), after the Babenberg Margraves had left Melk and before they moved permanently to Vienna. The Babenbergs built the Tulner Karner ossuary, a jewel of late Romanesque architecture (1240), which stands near to St Stefan parish church. This originally Romanesque church was added to in Gothic style around 1500 and baroqued in the 18th century. A Habsburg eagle over the doorway holds two Turkish heads in its mouth, celebrating the victory of Holy Roman Empire forces over the Ottoman Turks at the Battle of Vienna (1683).

For many centuries, frequent Danube floods threatened the town. This was abated by 19th-century hydrological works, which straightened the river behind flood dykes, but flooding was not finally prevented until the Greifenstein dam opened in 1984. Since then the Donaulände riverside promenade has been landscaped and a number of monuments have been erected in riverside gardens. One of these, the Mugln fountain, is composed of five columns of sandstone rocks that were removed from the riverbed, while another monument commemorates the *Nibelungenlied* epic tale.

STAGE 22
Tulln to Vienna

Start	Tulln, Nibelungen monument (175m)
Finish	Vienna, Schwedenplatz (164m)
Distance	37km
Waymarking	Donauradweg EV6 then Donaukanalradweg after Nussdorf

After Tulln the Danube turns south, where the valley narrows again as the river passes through the Wiener Pforte gap beneath the wooded hills of the Wienerwald. Another vast abbey is passed at Klosterneuburg. Riverside cycle tracks and quiet roads are used to reach the outskirts of Vienna, and then the Wien Donaukanal towpath is followed into the city centre. This stage is completely flat, except for climbing over bridges and flood dykes.

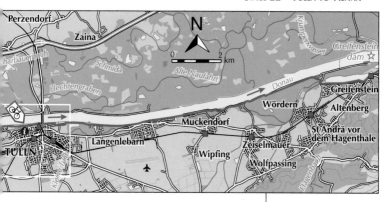

From **Nibelungen monument** in riverside gardens in Tulln, follow cycle track E parallel with the Danube. Pass in quick succession **Mugln fountain** (made of piles of flat stones) R, Donaubühne floating stage L and **statue of Roman Emperor Marcus Aurelius** R, then continue under girder bridge that takes both railway and road over Danube. Before marina, bear R away from river, then L and L again round marina to return to riverbank. Continue out of Tulln past Aubad lake R, dog-leg around small quay and past rear of houses at Rafelswörth, to reach **Langenlebarn** (5km, 174m) (accommodation, refreshments, station). Continue past Stromseidlung R and **Muckendorf marina** L (refreshments) to reach Greifenstein marina (refreshments).

map continues on page 191

At beginning of marina bear R away from river, fork R and R again, then turn L (Grenzweg) to pass **Greifenstein** village R. Continue alongside lagoon L with road becoming first Am Damm, then Am Sporn. Just before old harbour, turn R (Am Hafen) and where this bends R continue ahead away from river on cycle track. Follow this, bearing L to reach Greifenstein station (15km, 172m) (accommodation, refreshments, cycle shop, station).

In station car park, turn L (Kastanienallee) and continue parallel to railway on Donaulände with **Burg Greifenstein castle** R on hillside above. Turn L then R alongside lagoon and pass brightly decorated building R.

Turn L at T-junction (Strombaugelände) to reach Danube riverbank and bear R beside river. Continue on Donaustrasse past **Höflein** (17.5km, 167m) (station). After 700m, drop down L off road onto riverside cycle track, continuing past village and Silbersee R. Bear L (Am Durchstich) away from river beside drainage canal and continue between this canal L and railway behind houses R into **Kritzendorf** (20.5km, 169m) (accommodation, refreshments, station). Bear L to pass Kritzendorf station and where road ends continue ahead on cycle track beside drainage canal L.

Pass under curved road bridge, and while still under bridge, turn L across canal. Turn R on cycle track along opposite bank and continue along Am Durchstich into **Klosterneuburg** (24km, 167m) (accommodation, refreshments, camping, tourist office, cycle shop, station).

Klosterneuburg (pop. 25,000) is mainly a dormitory town for Vienna; indeed from 1938 to 1954 it was classified as a Viennese suburb. But it was not always this way. Once a Roman settlement, it was favoured by the Babenbergs in 1108, who constructed a Romanesque Augustinian abbey on the same site. This was extended in Gothic style in the 15th century. Between 1730 and 1755 the Habsburg Emperor Charles VI sponsored the building of the impressive baroque buildings that dominate the abbey today. On Charles' death, the imperial quarters in the abbey remained unfinished. For over 900 years, the abbey canons have fostered scholarship and collected art. As a result, the abbey and its churches are home to a series of notable artworks including the Verdun altar, which has 51 enamel panels.

Continue ahead at crossroads on cycle track beside In der Au, passing campsite L. Follow road around car park for **Happyland water park** R and continue past sports fields. Bear R into Strandbadstrasse, with wooded **Aupark** R and **Strandbad amusement park** L. Cross canal to reach T-junction and turn L (Donaustrasse) on cycle

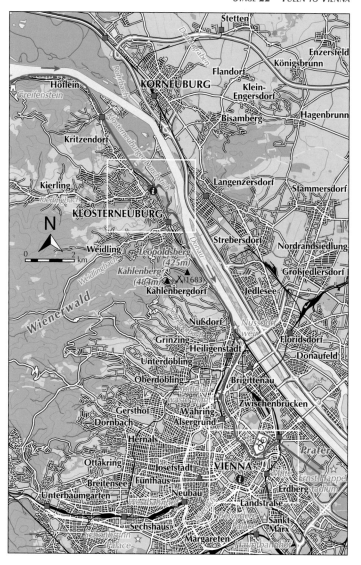

The Verdun altar is the most valuable of many artworks in Stift Klosterneuburg abbey

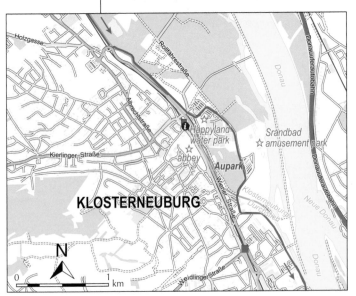

lane L of road. Bear R around back of barracks R and where road turns R, continue ahead at crossroads (still Donaustrasse) between industrial estate R and Danube L. Follow road bearing R and turn immediately L to pass sign showing beginning of Vienna. Fork R (Kuchelauer Hafenstrasse) and continue for 2km, winding between railway R and lagoon L, with wooded Wienerwald hills of Leopoldsberg (425m) and Kahlenberg (484m) rising R, to reach **Kahlenbergerdorf** (29km, 162m) (accommodation, refreshments, station).

> It was on the Kahlenberg, in the **Wienerwald hills**, that the decisive battle that lifted the siege of Vienna (1683) took place. The Turkish Ottoman army commanded by Mustapha Pasha was defeated by a combined force of troops from the Holy Roman Empire, under Charles of Lorraine, and the Polish Commonwealth, led by Jan III Sobieski, King of Poland. This victory of Christian forces over Islamic forces marked the end of the Turkish expansion into Europe and was hailed by the Catholic church as a major victory for Christendom. A huge picture of the battle, featuring Sobieski leading his Polish forces to victory, had pride of place outside the Sistine chapel in Rome's Vatican museum during the papacy of Pope John Paul II, who was Polish.
>
> The Weinviertel wine quarter, part of the Wienerwald, is home to extensive vineyards, with the south-facing slopes, overlooking Vienna, producing grapes that are used to make mostly young fresh white wine called heurige. The resulting wine can be drunk in *heurigerhausen* (local wine bars), particularly in Grinzing, Nussdorf and Kahlenbergdorf.

Where Kuchelauer Hafenstrasse ends, follow cycle track ahead beside railway and continue along Danube riverbank with landing stages for Danube cruise boats L. Cycle track continues underneath elevated motorway

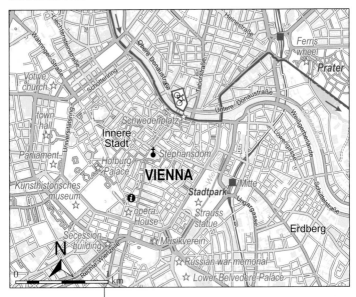

A very noticeable tower with a golden ball near its top is the chimney of Spittelau, Vienna's main waste incinerator.

entering the suburbs of Vienna passing **Nussdorf** R (31km, 163m) (refreshments, cycle shop, station).

Cycle track continues running under elevated motorway, passing **Nussdorf weir** and locks L at entrance to Wien Donaukanal. This canal is followed along towpath for 6km into centre of Vienna, passing **Heiligenstadt** R (refreshments, cycle shop, station). ◄

After passing a disused lock, fork R away from canal up a ramp onto Franz-Josefs-Kai by Salztorbrücke bridge. Continue along cycle path, crossing approach road of Marienbrücke bridge to reach **Schwedenplatz**, beside the quay for the hydrofoil service to Bratislava, in central **Vienna** (37km, 164m) (accommodation, refreshments, YH, camping, tourist office, cycle shop, station).

VIENNA

Vienna (pop. 1,750,000) is rightly regarded as one of Europe's greatest cities. As the imperial capital of the Habsburgs, it was endowed with many grand formal buildings, palaces, parks and boulevards. Despite losing its imperial position with the break-up of the Austro-Hungarian Empire in 1919, and transition to a new role as capital of one of the smaller European countries, it has retained its elegance and sense of imperial splendour.

The Romans chose the site (15BC) for Vindobona, one of their larger military camps guarding the Danube frontier. After the Romans left in the fifth century, there was a long period of decline until the Babenbergs moved the capital of the Öster Reich here from Klosterneuburg (1145). When the Habsburg dynasty moved in (1440), the city became the de facto capital of the Holy Roman Empire.

The huge Hofburg palace was the winter home of the Imperial family. The complex includes the *schatzkammer* (treasure chamber), which holds the crown jewels of the Holy Roman and Austro-Hungarian Empires, and the *hofreitschule* (Spanish Riding School), where Lipizzaner horses are trained and perform. In the western suburbs, the Schönbrunn palace, with its extensive gardens, was the Habsburgs' summer residence. The baroque Belvedere palace – the former home of Prince Eugene of Savoy – houses the Austrian art gallery, which includes paintings by Gustav Klimnt.

The broad Ringstrasse, following the line of the now demolished city walls, is lined with important buildings including the Austrian parliament, town hall and the Staatsoper opera house. The Kunsthistorisches museum, which has a huge collection of old master paintings, is one of the great art galleries of the world, while the Secession building is a fine example of *jugendstil* (art noveau) architecture. Vienna has a wide-ranging musical heritage and many celebrated composers have lived and worked in the city, including Mozart, Beethoven, Haydn, Bruckner, Mahler and Schubert, and many of them are buried in a special musician's corner in the *Zentralfriedhof* (Central cemetery). The city is closely associated with the works of Johann Strauss, a golden monument of whom can be found in the Stadtpark. On New Year's Eve the Pummerin bell of Stephansdom cathedral rings in the New Year for all of Austria, while on New Year's Day the Vienna Philharmonic's concert in the Musikverein concert hall is broadcast worldwide.

The southern frontage and gardens of Schönbrunn, summer palace of the Habsburgs

STAGE 23
Vienna to Bratislava

Start	Vienna, Schwedenplatz (164m)
Finish	Petržalka (Bratislava), Nový Most bridge (142m)
Distance	66.5km
Waymarking	Donauradweg EV6

After leaving Vienna through the Prater Gardens, the route crosses to the left bank of the Danube and mostly follows long straight flood dykes through the riparian wooded wetlands of the Donau-Auen national park. Recrossing the river before Hainburg, the route enters Slovakia to reach Petržalka, opposite the Slovak capital of Bratislava. Apart from a small ridge crossed after Hainburg, this stage is flat, and mostly follows riverbank cycle tracks or flood dykes, with only two short road sections.

From the S end of **Schwedenbrücke** beside Donaukanal in central Vienna, follow cycle track on L of Franz-Josef-Kai E to reach next bridge (Aspenbrücke). Turn L over

canal (cycle lane R of road) and continue ahead, bearing R into Praterstrasse. At huge Praterstern roundabout, turn R following cycle track around roundabout. Cross two approach roads and pass under railway bridge. Bear R into **Prater park and pleasure gardens**, with famous **Riesenrad Ferris wheel** L.

> The **Prater pleasure gardens** occupy land set aside by Emperor Maximillian II (1527–1576) as a private hunting ground. In 1766 Emperor Josef II opened the park for public enjoyment and allowed cafés and coffee houses to develop, although hunting continued until 1920. The Wurstelprater amusement park developed from these cafés and here you will find the Wiener Riesenrad.

map continues
on page 201

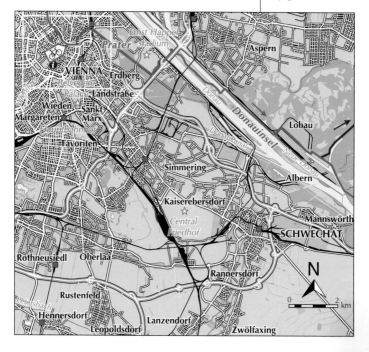

*The iconic Riesenrad
Ferris wheel in Prater gardens*

Built to celebrate the golden jubilee of Emperor Franz-Josef I in 1897, this 65m-high Ferris wheel was scheduled for demolition in 1916 but, due to lack of funds for this to be carried out, it survived and has since become an iconic symbol of Vienna. Apart from the wheel, there are fairground rides, shooting galleries, waxworks and traditional Viennese restaurants. Elsewhere in Prater are the *Wiener messe* (exhibition halls), the national stadium, a horseracing track and the Lilliputbahn railway for children.

Continue through Prater gardens on chestnut-lined Prater Hauptallee for 3km, passing **Ernst Happel Stadium** (Austian national stadium) L. At motorway overbridge turn L (Grünlandgasse) on cycle track underneath Austria's busiest motorway. Continue beside motorway then bear R and turn sharply R under slip road. Continue ahead climbing onto cycle track beside motorway over main channel of Danube. At end of bridge, follow cycle track L spiralling down to **Donauinsel**. ▸

Donauinsel is a 21km-long man-made island between the Danube and Neue Donau rivers, which was created between 1972 and 1988 as part of a flood prevention scheme.

Turn R and follow flood dyke along spine of island, passing under railway bridge and eventually bearing L (Steinspornbrücke bridge) to cross **Neue Donau**. Turn R at T-junction and continue alongside Neue Donau, passing a series of riverside bars and restaurants. ▸ Just before reaching colourful pontoon bridge on R, turn L across Raffineriestrasse into Lobgrundstrasse to reach **Lobau** (12km, 157m).

The beaches at the southern end of Neue Donau are popular with naturists. Do not be surprised to see naked people walking along the track.

Follow road bearing R between oil storage tanks (unsurfaced cycle track L). At end of refinery, bear L and R on cycle track beside Marchfelddamm flood dyke. ▸

With a couple of short diversions, this is followed for 32km to a point opposite Bad Deutsch.

Alternative route via Wittau

During periods of very high water levels, the route through Donau-Auen national park may be flooded between Lobau and Schönau. Signposted diversions, which add 5km to your journey, take you away from the river via **Wittau**.

For the main route, cross bridge over a side stream and continue alongside flood dyke into **Donau-Auen national park**.

The 93km² **Donau-Auen national park** was established in 1996 to protect the largest area of undeveloped wetland floodplain in central Europe, after environmentalists had succeeded in blocking construction of a hydro-electric dam at Hainburg, which would have flooded the area permanently. The park covers an area of backwaters, creeks and wooded swampland stretching for 38km along the Danube's banks – from Vienna to the Slovak border – and it is home to more than 30 species of mammal and 100 types of bird. The river runs freely at this point, with seasonal changes in water level of up to seven metres helping preserve the wetland nature of the environment. Detailed descriptions of the park habitat can be found at the visitor centre in Schloss Orth castle.

The route follows a cycle track along the Danube flood dyke through Donau-Auen national park

Approaching Schönau, asphalt ends and track becomes good-quality gravel. Where gravel ends and

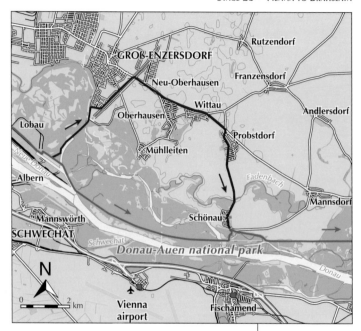

track ahead is unsurfaced, bear L on surfaced track over bridge through woods and continue for 500m to reach beginning of **Schönau** (23.5km, 151m) (refreshments). Turn R on another flood dyke. ▶ Follow flood dyke back to Marchfelddamm.

Continue ahead, now along flood dyke but some distance away from Danube, and after 7km cross a road that links **Orth** (1.5km L of track) (accommodation, refreshments) with riverbank restaurants at **Ufer** (1.2km R) (both 30.5km, 148m) (refreshments). Continue past turning for **Eckartsau** (37km, 147m) (accommodation, refreshments).

Where track along dyke ends, turn L on bridge over usually dry flood relief channel and R along flood dyke on opposite bank, passing **Stopfenreuth** (43.5km, 143m) (accommodation, refreshments). Pass under road bridge and immediately turn L and L again to pass over

map continues
on page 202

Alternative route
via Wittau rejoins
main route here.

201

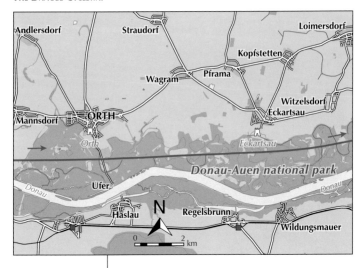

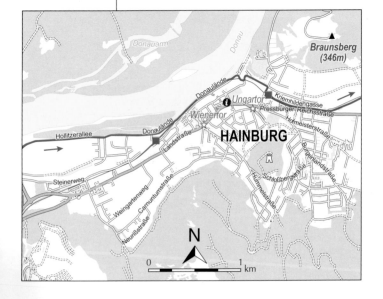

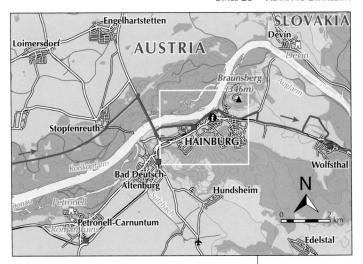

bridge (cycle track L of road). Continue over Danube on suspension bridge and 100m before reaching roundabout drop down L to reach road below bridge. Turn L (cycle track L) and then R across road into side road R. ▶ Continue on this road bearing R under Danube bridge and continue on Hollitzerallee, becoming Donaulände, into **Hainburg** (50km, 149m) (accommodation, refreshments, tourist office, station).

map continues on page 204

To reach **Bad Deutsch-Altenburg**, follow main road ahead.

Hainburg (pop. 6000) occupies one of the most strategically important locations on the Danube, literally the point where east meets west as, for many centuries, it was the most easterly point of the Holy Roman Empire. Sitting where wooded hills come down to the river on both banks, Hainburg was extensively fortified in the 15th century with 2.5km of walls, three city gates and 15 defensive towers. These defences, which still stand, are unrivalled in central Europe. They proved impenetrable until 1683, when the Turkish army advancing on Vienna stormed the city and killed 8432 residents. The most impressive gate, the Wienertor (1267), stands 31m high and was constructed with part of the funds received by Austria as ransom for the English King, Richard the Lionheart. It now houses the city museum.

Continue between Danube L and railway R passing **station** R and bear R on cycle track beside railway. Pass landing stage and emerge onto road. Immediately after water tower R, turn R under railway. Bear L and after 50m turn L back under railway. Follow road, bearing R into Nibelungengasse. Turn R (Krüklstrasse) and L before level crossing (Kriemhildengasse), parallel to railway past **Ungartor station** R. Continue ahead (Thebnerstrasse) out of Hainburg with Bratislava soon coming into view ahead. After 750m, turn sharply R on cycle track, then just before level crossing turn L beside railway. Pass recycling depot L, then after 800m turn L away from railway. Turn R at crossing of tracks, then bear R over small bridge on cobbled track into **Wolfsthal** (57.5km, 148m) (accommodation, refreshments, station).

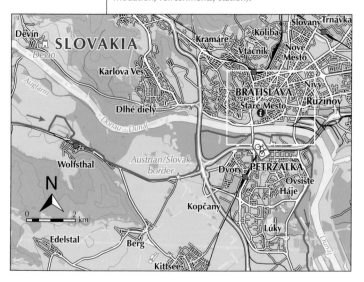

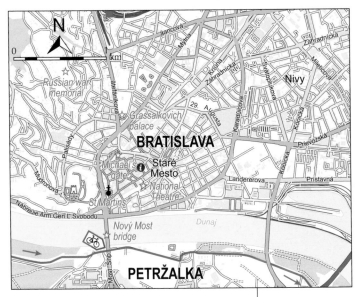

Turn L onto Haupstrasse and pass Schloss Walterskirchen castle L. Continue through village (no cycle lane) and towards end of built-up area, bear L onto cycle track that runs parallel to road, passing behind last few houses. Continue parallel to main road into open country and after 3km reach **Austrian–Slovak border** (62km, 139m). At this point the route crosses the old 'Iron Curtain'; all that is left of this once formidable barrier is a rusty blue gate that is left permanently open nowadays. Continue into Slovakia and follow cycle track as it bears L away from road to run parallel with motorway passing an old Soviet era bunker L. Bear R under motorway and continue along flood dyke with Danube L.

Emerge onto road (Viedenská cesta) and soon reach Nový Most suspension bridge in **Petržalka** (66.5km, 142m). A lift inside the bridge tower takes you to a view-ing gallery at the top for a fine view of the city. ▶

To reach **Bratislava** (accommodation, refreshments, YH, tourist office, cycle shop, station) on opposite bank, take ramp R up onto bridge and cross Danube into historic centre.

A viewing gallery and restaurant atop the Nový Most bridge in Bratislava

BRATISLAVA

Bratislava (pop. 460,000), previously known as Pressburg (German) and before that as Pozsony (Hungarian), is a vibrant and fast-developing city that has found a new purpose since the end of communism and the splitting of Slovakia from Czechoslovakia. For over 900 years (1000–1919), Pozsony was a Hungarian city. During the Turkish occupation of Hungary, when Budapest came under Ottoman control, the capital of Hungary moved to Pozsony and its castle became the residence of the Hungarian monarchy from 1536 to 1783. The city continued as an important regional centre during the period of the Austro-Hungarian Empire (1867–1919), with its central position between the imperial capitals of Budapest, Prague and Vienna aiding its commercial and industrial development. Its population was predominantly German (42 per cent) or Hungarian (41 per cent), with only 15 per cent Slovak, and the city was known by its German name Pressburg.

All this changed in 1919, when the Austro-Hungarian Empire was broken up by the Trianon Treaty and the new country of Czechoslovakia was established. Pressburg, together with much of Hungary north of the Danube, became Czechoslovak; its name changed to Bratislava, the language of government changed to Czech and many of its Hungarian residents left. After the Second World War, the German-speaking population was expelled, and Czechoslovakia came under Soviet control with a communist government. The concentration on heavy industry and the construction of large numbers of state-owned residential blocks to house Slovaks moving from rural areas gave the city a polluted environment and a rather grim countenance. The old city centre became neglected and run down. The end of communism (1989) and Slovak independence (1992) resulted in Bratislava becoming capital of the new country of Slovakia. Economic recovery was slow at first, but entry into the European Union (2004) and Bratislava's close proximity to western European markets attracted substantial investment in new industry. The city centre has since been substantially renovated. In 2009 economic success led to Slovakia becoming the first ex-Soviet block country to be admitted into the Euro currency zone.

The two dominant landmarks in the city are Schloss Hrad castle and Nový Most suspension bridge. The castle stands on a plateau, 85m above the old town. Formerly the site (successively) of a Celtic acropolis, a Roman camp and a Slavic fortress, the first stone castle was built in the 10th century. The current design dates from remodelling during the reign of Maria Theresa, although a fire in 1811 destroyed most of the building, which then lay in ruins until the late 20th century. Recent renovations have returned the castle to its Habsburg style, with the brightly white painted edifice visible from miles around. The strikingly elegant Nový Most bridge over the Danube was built during the communist era and it was originally called the Bridge of the Slovak National Uprising. Its single suspension tower, topped by an iconic restaurant and viewing gallery, is often used as a symbol for the city.

Other important buildings in the old town include the Gothic St Martin's cathedral (formerly the coronation church for Hungarian kings), town hall, Michael's gate and National Theatre. The baroque-style Grassalkovich palace is now the presidential residence, while the old bishop's palace is the seat of the Slovak government. One highly regarded sculpture is *Cumil the Peeper*, a furtive figure emerging from a manhole, said to be trying to look up ladies' skirts.

STAGE 24
Bratislava to Mosonmagyaróvár

Start	Petržalka (Bratislava), Nový Most bridge (139m)
Finish	Mosonmagyaróvár, Schloss Óvár castle (122m)
Distance	37km
Waymarking	EV6 (intermittent)

Below Bratislava the Danube divides into a number of channels between the main river, which has been channelled behind high dykes into a large lake above the Gabčikovo dam, and the Mosoni Duna (Little Danube), which meanders widely through the Szigetköz, an area of mostly drained former wetland. After leaving Bratislava, this route soon enters Hungary. Turning away from the rather sterile banks of the impounded Danube, it follows a cycle track beside a main road directly to Mosonmagyaróvár.

There are a number of alternative routes through this area, and it is possible to stay in Slovakia by following the Danube from Bratislava all the way to Komárno (Stage 26). One such alternative starts in Čunovo, first following the high dykes impounding water behind the Gabčikovo dam, then crossing the river and using long stretches of unsurfaced track. Bratislava to Komárno is 106km by this route (compared to 130km by the route through Hungary described below and continued in Stages 25–26), but there are no towns of any size and tourist infrastructure is under-developed.

From under S side of **Nový Most suspension bridge** in Petržalka, head E on cycle track beside Viedenská cesta. Turn L following green asphalt cycle lane and bear R *This turn is easy to miss.* parallel with Danube. ◄ Continue ahead on cycle track along flood dyke and pass under road bridge. Follow flood dyke under motorway bridge and past tennis club R. Continue alongside main road R then follow flood dyke bearing away from road. Drop down R below dyke (path along dyke is for pedestrians). Briefly rejoin dyke to pass sewerage works R. By sewerage works, zigzag R and L again onto cycle track along old road between fields R and drainage canal L, still running parallel to flood dyke, and follow this for 10km, passing **Rusovce** R. ▶

At point where route reaches road serving Čunovo sluice and locks (visible L), turn immediately R through barrier and between trees to reach **Čunovo village** (17.5km, 130m) (accommodation, refreshments, camping).

Turn L in village (Na hrádzi) and first R (Ražná Ulica). At dual-carriageway street (Hraničiarska Ulica) with village green down centre, turn L and continue out of village between fields on Schengenská. After passing adventure playground L, continue across **Slovak–Hungarian border** (no border post) into Hungarian town of **Rajka** (21km, 130m) (accommodation, refreshments, camping, station).

Turn R at crossroads (Petőfi Sándor utca) and just after passing childrens' playground on R, turn L (Kiss János utca). Turn R at third crossroads (Táncsics Mihály

This is a popular cycle excursion for Bratislavans and it can be very busy, particularly at weekends; there are refreshment stalls beside the track.

map continues on page 210

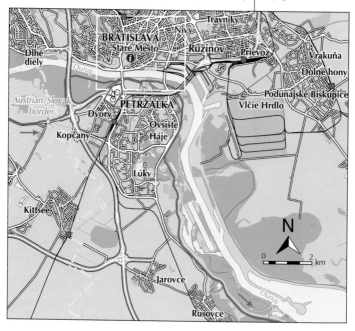

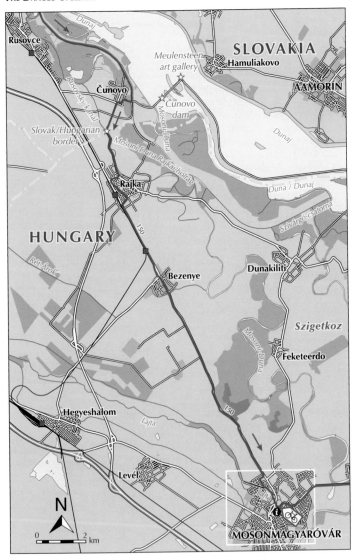

utca) and just before reaching main road, join cycle track L. Follow this across main road and turn L on cycle track beside road (route 150), which is followed for 3km to reach beginning of **Bezenye** (26km, 125m). Where cycle track ends, continue ahead on service road, soon returning to cycle track beside main road, which continues through village and on through open country for 8km to reach beginning of Mosonmagyaróvár.

Just past car dealership R, turn R (Orgona utca) and first L (Kadocsa Gyula utca). At end bear L alongside canal (Kishíd utca) then turn R over canal bridge. Pass high school R to reach junction with main road with Óvár castle visible ahead. Bear R on cycle track beside main road then after 50m, just before reaching bridge over branch of **river Lajta**, turn L across road onto Vár Kőz running parallel to the Lajta. Follow this to reach end of stage by main entrance to Schloss Óvár castle in **Mosonmagyaróvár** (37km, 122m) (accommodation, refreshments, camping, tourist office, cycle shop, station).

Mosonmagyaróvár (pop. 32,500) was originally two separate towns – Moson and Magyaróvár – but they merged in 1939. It was an important medieval trading centre on the route between Hungary and Austria, with an ancient castle first built in 1009. Rebuilt and

The Mosoni Duna river winds through the Szigetköz between Bratislava and Győr

The pedestrianised Magyar utca in Mosonmagyaróvár

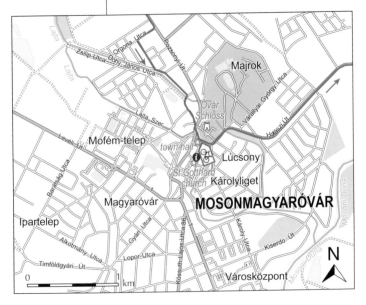

modernised a number of times, it achieved its current form in 1810. Nowadays the castle, which houses an agricultural university, and part of the old town have been restored as heritage-listed buildings. The river Lajta flows through the town in a number of channels, crossed in total by 17 bridges.

The reopening of trading links since the fall of communism has led to a boom in dentistry. With 350 practitioners, the town has the highest number of dentists per head in the world. Clients are attracted not only from nearby Austria, where dental treatment is considerably more expensive than in Hungary, but also from worldwide, flying in via Vienna and Bratislava airports.

STAGE 25
Mosonmagyaróvár to Győr

Start	Mosonmagyaróvár, Schloss Óvar castle (122m)
Finish	Győr, Széchenyi tér (120m)
Distance	40.5km
Waymarking	EV6

This stage doesn't have any views of the Danube. The route continues to head south-west through the Szigetköz plain between the Danube and Mosoni Duna rivers. The whole stretch follows a cycle track beside a country road, passing through a series of villages.

From outside main entrance to **Schloss Óvár castle** in Mosonmagyaróvár, head E on Csernáti Sándor utca (cycle track R). Continue beside Halászi út out of town and through open country, then cross Mosoni Duna into **Halászi** (5km, 121m) (accommodation, refreshments, camping).

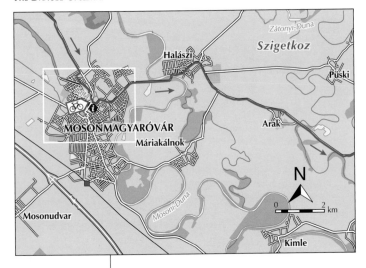

Follow cycle track beside main road (Kossuth Lajos utca) through town. Pass St Márton church L and follow road bearing R (Púski utca) into open country. Continue past **Arak** R to reach **Darnózseli** (14km, 116m) (refreshments).

At beginning of village, cycle track switches to L of road and back to R as road leaves village. Continue beside road to Hédervár. Entering village, where road

Hédervár castle is now a luxury hotel

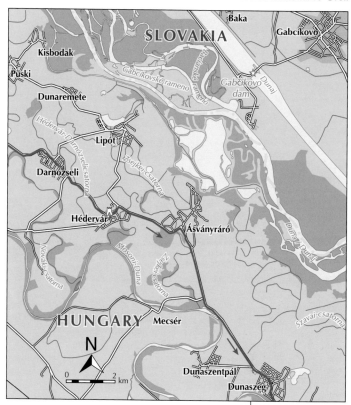

turns sharply L, pass fortified **castle** in park L and continue into **Hédervár** (17.5km, 120m) (accommodation, refreshments).

Cycle through village on cycle lane, passing church L and bearing R into open country. After village, cycle track recommences and continues until beginning of **Ásványráró** (21km, 114m) (accommodation, refreshments).

Cycle on cycle lane on main road (Győri út) bearing L to reach roundabout beside church. ▶ Turn R at roundabout and follow road out of town on cycle track R.

map continues
on page 216

To reach centre of Ásványráró, continue straight ahead at roundabout.

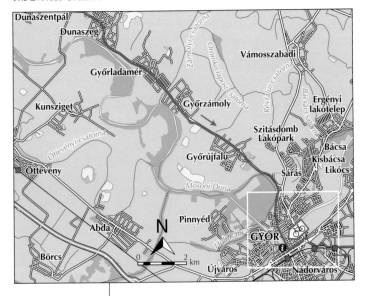

Continue through open country, passing alongside bend of Mosoni Duna R, to reach **Dunaszeg** (28.5km, 113m) (accommodation, refreshments).

Cycle on poor-quality cycle lane straight through village to reach Mosoni Duna, where cycle track restarts, and continue beside road, parallel with river R, into **Győrladamér** and then **Győrzámoly** (accommodation, refreshments). After short stretch of open country, reach **Győrújfalu** (36km, 110m) (refreshments). In village, by small square with churches on both sides of road, bear R on cycle track away from road. Cross next street and follow cycle track back to main road. After another stretch of open country, join flood dyke and pass wooded area alongside an old course of Mosoni Duna.

Just before beginning of Győr, follow cycle track, forking R alongside Hédervári út with old river course R. At point where houses begin on R, cycle track switches to L of road. At busy road junction, with university R, follow cycle track ahead across roundabout into Rónay

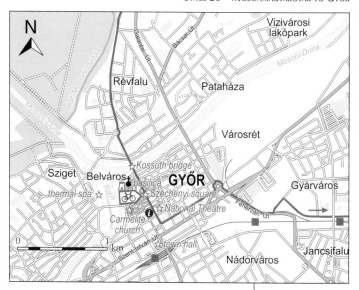

Győr town hall

Jácint utca (cycle lane R). Continue over Mosoni Duna on **Kossuth hid girder bridge** (cycle lane L). Once over bridge, go straight ahead along pedestrian precinct (Jedlik Anyos utca) to reach Széchenyi tér square L, in centre of **Győr** (40.5km, 120m) (accommodation, refreshments, camping, tourist office, cycle shop, station).

GYŐR

Győr (pop. 132,000) sits by the confluence of the Mosoni Duna and Rába rivers and is the regional capital of north-west Hungary. Hungarian people first arrived here in about AD900, occupying an abandoned Roman fortress on Káptalandomb hill by the river junction. Over the centuries this fortress was strengthened and extended, mainly to defend against increasing Turkish threats, eventually becoming Hungary's largest castle. Much of Győr's defensive walls were demolished during the 19th century to provide building materials as the city expanded.

The nearby *basilika* (cathedral) is a mix of styles from the 11th to the 19th centuries, a result of rebuilding after destruction incurred during Turkish occupation. Inside the Ladislaus chapel the Hermes is displayed, a gold-plated silver reliquary holding the skull of St Ladislaus. Below the hill is

The golden Hermes bust in Győr cathedral contains the skull of St Ladislaus

the Carmelite church, which has a magnificent yellow baroque façade, while the Benedictine church on Széchenyi tér square has two white towers. Nearby is the ultra-modern *Nemzeti Színház* (National Theatre). The city prospered as ship-borne trade on the river developed, and later attracted industry when the railway arrived. During the immediate post-Second World War period, with communists in power, many of the historic buildings were neglected. This changed in the 1970s, so much so that in 1989 Győr won a European award for its protection of historic monuments.

Post-communist developments have seen Audi build a large car factory just east of the city, which produces two million car engines annually and assembles some Audi sports cars. Ninety per cent of all Audi engines are made here, as well as some for Volkswagen and Lamborghini.

STAGE 26
Győr to Komárom

Start	Győr, Széchenyi tér (120m)
Finish	Komárom roundabout (113m)
Distance	53km
Waymarking	EV6

After Győr, the Mosoni Duna turns north to rejoin the Danube. This route leaves the river to head east through gently rolling countryside, crossing and recrossing a low ridge, before turning north to rejoin the Danube at Komárom. There is a mixture of field tracks, country roads and cycle tracks, with some stretches of main road without cycle lanes.

From **Széchenyi tér square** in Győr, follow pedestrianised Czuczor Gergely utca south, passing Nemzeti Szinház (**national theatre**) L. One street before reaching dual carriageway, turn L (Árpád út) and follow this to reach large roundabout. Follow cycle track clockwise (ie wrong way) around outside of this roundabout and leave by third exit (**Fehérvári út**) on cycle track L of road. ▸

The route out of Győr is complicated and street names are often not displayed. Follow directions carefully.

Pass under road bridge and continue past retail park L. At traffic lights, turn L (Vágóhid utca) across railway track and first R (Kandó utca). Follow cycle track beside road through industrial area and past **Győr Gyárváros station** R. Continue parallel with railway R and stay on cycle track as road bears L. After 150m, turn R (Hűtőház utca) and follow this on cycle track R through industrial area to reach crossroads with traffic lights. ▸

The road on the left leads to the Audi car engine factory.

Continue ahead out of Győr on cycle track (now L of road) and follow this bearing L between fields. Pass large poultry farm R and continue alongside new road serving Audi factory to reach roundabout. Follow cycle track beside road to reach beginning of **Győrszentiván** (8.5km, 113m) (refreshments, station).

Turn R at roundabout (Egressy utca). Dogleg R and L across next junction, then turn L (Pince utca) and immediately R (Kenderes utca) past cemetery R. Continue into Vasút ut, bearing L parallel to railway and passing **Győrszentiván station** R. At end of village, turn R over level crossing, then L and R climbing steadily through ribbon development of **Nagyhegy**.

This track can be muddy when wet.

After end of houses, bear L and R on unsurfaced track to cross motorway bridge. ◄ Continue on rough unsurfaced track between fields L and woods R into **Szőlőhegy** (16.5km, 149m).

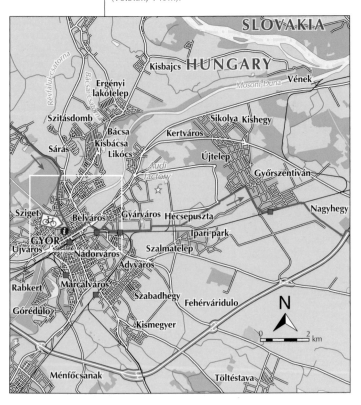

Simple church bell tower in Nagyhegy village

map continues on page 222

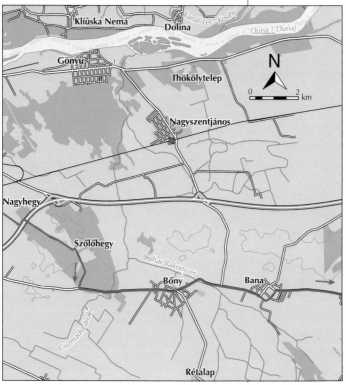

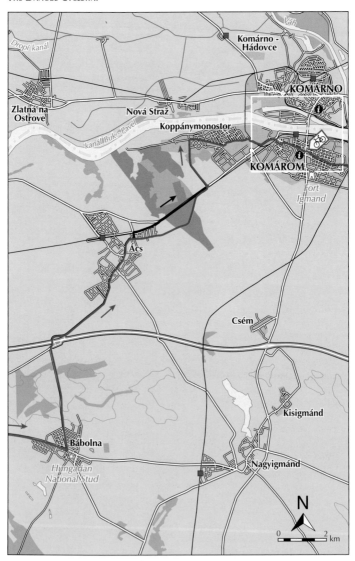

Turn L and R in village and continue on road out of village and through woods, dropping downhill. After 1.75km, turn L at T-junction and follow road into **Bőny** (22km, 123m) (refreshments). Pass through village on Szabadság utca. ▶

Continue on main road to reach **Bana** (26km, 126m) (accommodation, refreshments).

Where road bears L by Coop supermarket, keep straight ahead (Petőfi Sándor utca). Fork L and then bear L (József Attila utca). Continue to T-junction and turn R (Mártirok útja). Follow road out of village and between fields into **Bábolna** (30.5km, 133m) (accommodation, refreshments).

Bábolna (pop. 4000) owes its early existence to being a stop-over point on the drove road by which cattle and horses from the Hungarian plains were herded to market in Austria. This early connection with animal livestock led to the foundation of a horse breeding and stud farm in 1789, established to provide horses and cattle for the Hungarian army. In 1836 an Arabian stallion named Shagya was imported from Syria and this horse became the progenitor of a breed of thoroughbreds now recognised all over Europe. In addition to the stud, a military riding academy was established and Bábolna became a centre of equine activity. The complex of buildings, which today thrives as the Hungarian National Stud, can be visited. These include the indoor riding school, stud yard and stables, coach museum and horse museum. Guests can stay at the old Imperial Guest House, located in the historical stud yard. Of over 250 horses stabled here, 19 are breeding stallions.

Turn sharply L at roundabout in middle of Bábolna (Ácsi út) and follow this road out of town into open country. Climb back over same ridge that was crossed earlier, then descend to cross motorway bridge. Bear R, briefly beside motorway, passing motorway service area R

EV6 turns left 2km after Bőny and follows a longer and more westerly route via Nagyszentjános to Ács, which includes 3km of rough unsurfaced track.

(refreshments), and continue through fields to reach **Ács** (40km, 117m) (refreshments, camping, station).

Continue through very spread out town on main road (Komáromi utca). Towards end of town, where main road turns L to cross railway, continue straight ahead into Kossuth Lajos utca.

Alternative route avoiding rough track

Track beyond Ács is in very poor condition and becomes muddy after wet weather. For alternative route (on busy main road) turn L over railway and R to join main road after 1km. This alternative rejoins main route after 4km.

Where Kossuth Lajos utca ends at a turning circle, main route continues ahead on unsurfaced cycle track between fields. Follow this into woods, eventually emerging onto farm road. Continue beside railway and turn L over level crossing. Dogleg R and L over main road. ◄ Bear R onto quiet country road leading to **Koppánymonostor** (47.5km, 120m) (accommodation, refreshments).

Alternative route from Ács rejoins main route here.

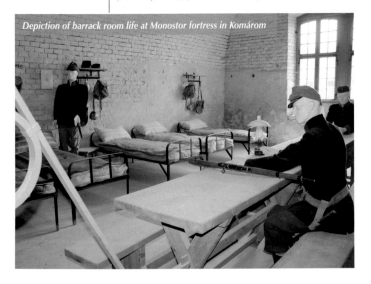

Depiction of barrack room life at Monostor fortress in Komárom

Turn R at T-junction (Koppány Vezér út) and follow this road through village. At crossroads, where houses on R end, join cycle track R and follow this beside road out of village. Cross railway level crossing and turn L at T-junction on cycle track R of main road (Ácsi út) passing entrance to **Fort Monostor** L.

Monostor, one of three military forts ringing Komárom, is the largest modern-era fortification in central Europe, covering an area of over 70ha and possessing barracks for 8000 soldiers. Built between 1850 and 1871, during the period of the Austro-Hungarian Empire, its main purpose was to control shipping on the Danube. Despite its impressive system of walls, ditches and casements, the fortress never saw military action and was mostly used as a training garrison. During the Soviet period it was used as a secret arsenal to store large quantities of Russian weapons and ammunition.

Cross another level crossing and turn immediately R (Zrinyi Miklós utca). Turn first L and L again at T-junction by retirement home. Turn R at next T-junction onto cycle track beside main road to reach roundabout in centre of **Komárom** (53km, 113m) (accommodation, refreshments, camping, tourist office, cycle shop, station). ▶

To reach Komárno (Slovakia), turn L at roundabout and follow road over Danube bridge.

Komárom and Komárno, sister towns across the Danube, were part of the same Hungarian community prior to the break-up of the Austro-Hungarian Empire in 1919. Indeed, Komárno, on the north bank, was the main centre of activity and Komárom (then called Újszőny) was a sleepy village. From 1919 until 2007, customs and immigration checks slowed connections across the river, but since both Slovakia and Hungary signed the Schengen accord in 2007 all restrictions have been lifted. Even today, 60 per cent of the population of Komárno are ethnically Hungarian.

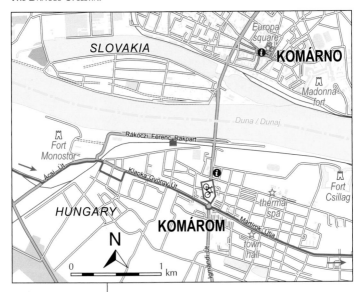

In earlier times the combined city was a major Hungarian military centre, ringed by defensive bastions as well as being the headquarters of a naval flotilla on the Danube. During the Hungarian revolution (1848–1849), it was the last city to be recaptured by Austria. Komárom has little of interest except for its three defensive fortresses: Csillag, Igmánd and Monostor (east, south and west of the town, respectively). By contrast, the centre of Komárno has a number of historic buildings. Komárno's main industry is shipbuilding, and it produces many of the vessels that ply the Danube.

STAGE 27
Komárom to Esztergom

Start	Komárom roundabout (113m)
Finish	Esztergom basilica (109m)
Distance	52.5km
Waymarking	EV6

Although following the Danube, this stage is seldom on the riverbank. In fact, although close by, the main stream of the river is hardly visible. Mostly following a main road – usually on a cycle track, but not always – this is the most exposed stage of all, in terms of encountering traffic. The route skirts the end of a range of hills that stretches down to the river, and is generally flat.

From **Komárom roundabout**, continue east on Mártirok útca (cycle track L of road) passing yellow church L and predominantly orange **town hall** R. Cross railway level crossing by small station R and cycle through **Szőny** (4km, 111m) (accommodation, camping, station).

map continues on page 228

Pass through village on Szőnyi út, which becomes Széchenyi István utca then Petőfi Sándor utca (cycle lane R). Where houses end on L, cycle track switches to L and continues over level crossing. Pass Soviet era residential estate at **Nagykolónia** and derelict **aluminium factory**, both L, before reaching **Almásfüzitő** (11km, 110m) (station), where cycle track ends.

The Soviet era **aluminium factory**, Almásfüzitő, was the largest in central Europe. It operated from 1950 until 1997 and employed 2300 people producing a total of 10 million tonnes of aluminium oxide from bauxite ore. A typical brutalist frieze above the front entrance shows patriotic workers and the message 'work for us is a matter of honour and duty'. The tailing ponds, where red oxide waste was dumped, take up a large area between the main road and the Danube. The EU is providing funds to clean up this highly toxic site.

Continue on busy main road past chemical works and cross drainage canal and railway. Fork L on quieter road parallel to railway with wooded hills R closing in ahead, to reach **Dunaalmás** (accommodation, refreshments, camping, station), which merges directly

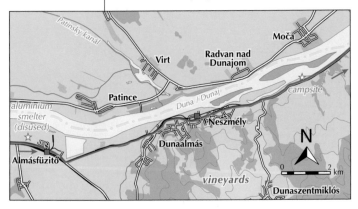

Süttő church

into wine-producing village of **Neszmély** (18km, 117m) (accommodation, refreshments, camping, station).

map continues
on page 230

Pass through village into open country with vineyard covered slopes R. Cross railway level crossing and continue with railway R and a Danube side arm L. Pass riverside campsite L (accommodation, refreshments, camping).

Emerge onto riverbank and follow road into **Süttő** (25.5km, 111m) (refreshments, station).

A number of **quarries** producing high-quality building stone are situated in the hills south of Süttő. Süttő stone was used in many of Hungary's most important buildings, including Esztergom basilica, Visegrád palace, Szeged cathedral, and both the Hungarian Parliament building and St Matthias church in Budapest.

Follow road away from riverbank across railway and gently uphill through centre of village. Pass industrial area in **Piszke** L to reach **Lábatlan** (29.5km, 118m) (accommodation, refreshments, station).

Continue through village, passing cement works and an industrial area L. Cycle track resumes R of road and continues into **Nyergesújfalu** (35km, 108m) (refreshments, station).

In middle of town cycle track ends and it is necessary to turn R (Béke tér), then follow road bearing L and turn R again to rejoin main street. Continue through town on cycle track R, then cross railway level crossing and continue between road L and railway R through open country.

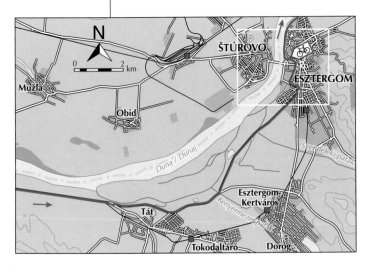

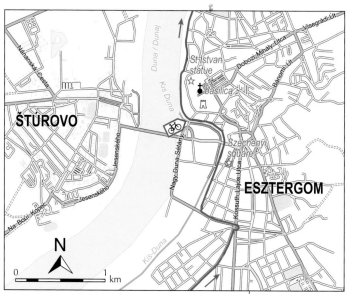

At beginning of **Tát** village (40.5km, 107m) (accommodation, refreshments, station), where road forks, cycle track crosses to L of road, then follows L fork to bypass the village. Continue along flood dyke for 5km. passing Tatito beach resort L, to reach road junction. Fork L and cycle on road, with green cupola of Esztergom basilica visible ahead to reach Esztergom. ▶

Care is needed as this is a busy, narrow road with no cycle lane.

Turn L at roundabout (Árok utca) and continue to reach canal bridge. Turn R before bridge (Kis Duna sétány), then immediately L and R alongside canal and continue past two bridges. Stage ends at third bridge (Kossuth Lajos hid), immediately below **Esztergom basilica** R, which sits on hill-top 50m above the river (52.5km, 109m) (accommodation, refreshments, YH, camping, cycle shop, station).

ESZTERGOM

Esztergom (pop. 31,000) is one of Hungary's oldest cities. Palaeolithic remains have been found on Castle Hill and the Romans built a fortified settlement here. With the arrival of the Magyars, Esztergom became the country's capital and in 1000 the first Hungarian King, István I, was crowned here. The royal palace and castle chapel were built during the reign of Bela IV (1235–1270).

Esztergom castle dates from the reign of Bela IV in the 13th century

However, a Mongol invasion in 1249 caused the royal court to move to Buda, with the city losing its position as national capital. The Catholic archbishop moved into the empty royal palace and the city became the centre of Catholic faith in Hungary.

Turkish occupation during the 15th and 16th centuries left Esztergom in ruins. Recovery was slow until the building of the basilica (1822–1869) reinvigorated the city. Standing atop caste hill, this cathedral – the biggest church in the country – dominates the surrounding countryside. It was consecrated in 1856, with Franz Liszt composing a special mass for the ceremony. The basilica contains a number of important architectural elements. The Renaissance Bakócz chapel was actually rebuilt inside the basilica from its original location in Süttő, while the altarpiece in the choir, painted by Grigoletti and based on Titian's *Assumption of the Virgin* in Venice, is claimed to be the largest in the world. The dome can be visited for outstanding views. Esztergom's role as the seat of the Catholic primate and centre of the church in Hungary earned it the contrasting sobriquets 'Hungary's Rome', from believers, and 'city of reaction', from communist authorities.

The city was badly damaged during the Second World War and the impressive Maria Valeria Bridge, which connects Esztergom and Stúrovo over the Danube, was destroyed. Remaining in ruins for decades, it was not reopened until 2001. Since the Schengen accord, the bridge nowadays provides barrier-free access to Slovakia.

STAGE 28
Esztergom to Szentendre

Start	Esztergom basilica (109m)
Finish	Szentendre, promenade (105m)
Distance	48km
Waymarking	EV6

This stage, the most attractive of the Hungarian stages, sees the river curve south, cutting through a narrow gap between wooded mountains known as the Danube Bend. The route crosses by ferry to the left bank to avoid sections of busy road, then recrosses to visit Visegrád and end at the artists' town of Szentendre.

On riverside promenade, immediately below **Esztergom basilica**, follow riverside cycle track N alongside Danube for 6km. Turn L on main road (no cycle lane) and continue through **Búbánatvölgy** (7km, 109m) (accommodation).

Follow main road through village and away from river, passing through hamlet of Basaharc to reach road junction after 3.5km.

Alternative route via main road
Continuing ahead takes you directly to Visegrád, cycling through **Pilismarót** and **Dömös** on busy main road (3km shorter than main route).

For the main route, turn L to reach Szobi *rév* (**ferry**) (accommodation, refreshments, camping). Cross Danube by ferry (departures 50mins past every hr) to **Szob** (12.5km, 105m) (refreshments, station). Immediately beyond landing stage turn R on cycle track beside river. Cross bridge over side stream and continue on undulating track first between railway L and river R then bearing R to run between main road L and river R.

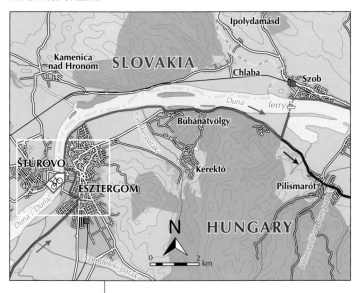

Visegrád stands beside an attractive stretch of river known as the Danube Bend

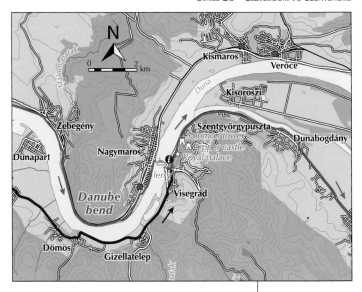

Pass through **Zebegény** (17km, 110m) (accommodation, refreshments, station), where route bears away
briefly R from main road onto quiet street between
houses, then continue to Dömösi Átkelés. Continue
round long sweeping bend L, where wooded hills of the
Danube Bend come right down to riverside on both sides
of river, eventually moving away from road with Visegrád
castle coming into view high above opposite bank. Cycle
track emerges onto promenade to reach **Nagymaros ferry
ramp** (accommodation, refreshments, station). Cross river
by ferry (departures hourly on hr) to **Visegrád** (25.5km,
103m) (accommodation, refreshments, camping, tourist
office, cycle shop).

map continues
on page 237

At end of ferry approach, turn L and R across main
road away from river into Rév utca. ▶ Turn L in front of
church (Fő utca) and pass **royal palace complex** R and
continue with mountain-top Visegrád castle high above
R. At end of built-up area, bear L and turn R onto main

Alternative route
via Pilismarót and
Dömös rejoins
main route here.

VISEGRÁD CASTLE

The ruins of Visegrád castle sit on a hilltop high above the Danube bend, at a point where the river breaks through the final mountain barrier before it reaches the Hungarian plain. This strategic position was first used by the Romans as a key point on the Limes defensive line along the Danube. After they departed, local chieftains expanded and developed the castle until it was destroyed during the Mongol invasions. The current fortress was started by King Bela IV in 1246 and it soon became a stronghold of the Hungarian kings. It consisted of an upper castle on top of a 328m-high hill, a lower castle on a subsidiary hill and a bastion beside the river, all of which were connected by defensive walls. Later, a royal palace was constructed on the banks of the Danube, terraced into the side of the hill and separate from the castle. After the royal court moved to Buda, the palace continued in use as a summer residence. The small town of Visegrád (pop. 1700) grew up to serve this palace. The whole complex fell into disrepair following the 16th-century Turkish occupation. Restoration began in 1871 and continued until 1964. Little regard was given to historical accuracy and some of the work was undertaken in concrete. The remains of the royal palace were rediscovered in 1935.

Although it is possible to visit the upper castle (and this is the most popular destination for car- and coach-borne tourists), it is a tough 5km uphill slog from the town. A better way to spend your time and energy may be to visit the lower castle and the ruins of the royal palace, where the red marble Lions Fountain is the main attraction.

road, pass leisure boat landing stage, then leave Visegrád through archway.

Cycle on main road (no cycle lane) for 3km, past small ferry serving **Szentendrei Sziget island**. After 1km, just after a small bar L, cycle track sign directs you L onto cycle track that runs beside river behind houses in **Dunabogdány** (31.5km, 103m) (accommodation, refreshments, camping). At end of village, cycle track turns R away from river and L alongside main road (cycle rack L of road). Pass under road bridge into open country. After 2.5km, cycle track ends and you continue on main road (no cycle lane) to reach **Tahitótfalu** (38km, 104m) (accommodation, refreshments, camping, cycle shop).

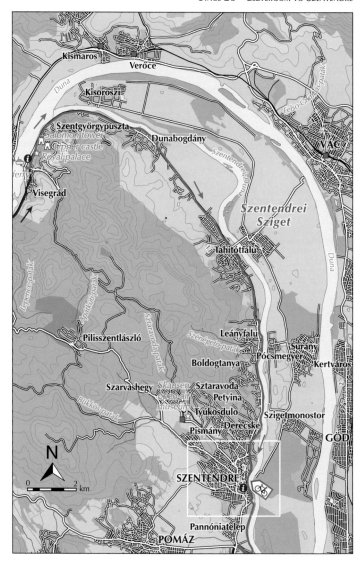

Continue through town to reach beginning of Leányfalu. Pass set back bus stop L and take next turn L, beside campsite L, onto a cycle track leading towards river. ◄ Follow cycle track winding through trees parallel to river. Pass swimming pool complex R and bear L past pedestrian ferry pier L in **Leányfalu** (42km, 105m) (accommodation, refreshments, camping).

This turn is easy to miss.

Continue parallel to river, rejoining main road at end of village. Follow cycle track beside road for 400m, then bear L onto cycle track that runs along behind houses, again parallel to river. Pass vehicular ferry and after 2.5km go through barrier, bear L on small road, then bear L alongside main road.

At next road junction, fork L (Korniss Dezsö sétány becoming Duna korzó) with cycle track L. Where cycle track ends continue on Danube promenade (Duna Korzó) into centre of **Szentendre** (48km, 105m) (accommodation, refreshments, camping, tourist office, station).

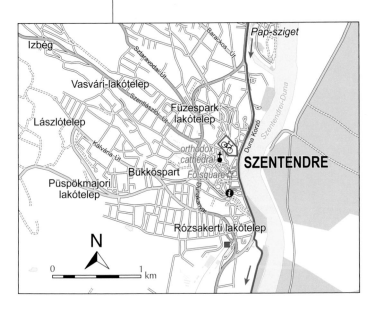

Szentendre (pop. 26,000), well-known for its collection of craft workshops, studios and art galleries, which draw coachloads of tourists from Budapest, was a centre of Serbian immigration into Hungary between the 17th and the 19th centuries. Leaving their own country to escape Turkish occupation, these Serbs brought Christian orthodox churches and colourful baroque merchants' houses to Szentendre. After the Trianon Treaty most of Hungary's Serbs emigrated to Yugoslavia and today there are less than 100 ethnic Serbs living in the town. Nevertheless, there are still seven orthodox churches and a museum of Serbian orthodox heritage.

Skanzen open-air ethnographical museum can be found 3km north-west of Szentendre. Taking its name from similar museums in Scandinavia, Skanzen was established in 1967 to collect examples of rural architecture and lifestyles from across Hungary. Original buildings, including mills, farms and churches, have been

Bogdányi utca in Szentendre is lined with artisans' workshops and galleries

239

transported to the site and reconstructed in 10 village groups, which are joined together by a tram that takes visitors from village to village.

STAGE 29
Szentendre to Budapest

Start	Szentendre, promenade (105m)
Finish	Budapest chain bridge (104m)
Distance	24km
Waymarking	EV6

This final short stage into the Hungarian capital is mostly on dedicated cycle tracks along the right bank of the Danube. The Buda Hills – a leafy suburban dormitory and forested recreation area – rise to the west, while a series of linear islands, including Margitsziget (Margaret Island), can be found in the river. The final entry into Budapest passes the neo-gothic parliament building across the river to end below the city's historic collection of buildings, including the royal palace, on Castle Hill.

Leaving Szentendre, follow the promenade (**Duna Korzó**) S. Cross small bridge and continue on cycle track L of road. Just past tennis courts L, where car park starts, turn L on cycle track that winds back to riverside and continues along flood dyke. Pass military ordnance depot R where there is an old Soviet ground to air missile and launcher beside the fence. Turn R alongside small creek. Follow this for 800m away from Danube, then turn L to cross creek at first bridge. The next 2.5km is a rough track that can be difficult in wet weather.

Alternative route avoiding rough track
Alternative route uses cycle track R of main road for 4km then turns L back to riverbank.

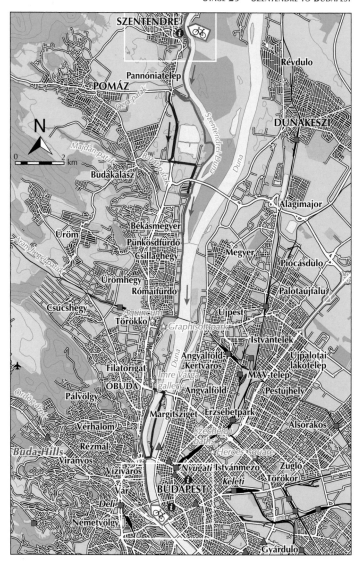

For main route, immediately after bridge turn L through barrier and follow opposite side of creek back towards river. Fork L in woods below flood dyke on unsurfaced track through forest. Where this ends climb up R onto dyke and continue on gravel track, which becomes rough asphalt road. When this reaches some buildings R, turn L on easily missed brick block track dropping down off dyke into woods and follow this bearing R alongside Danube to reach houses and a small ferry (8km, 103m) (refreshments).

Continue along riverside cycle track under motorway bridge to reach a drainage canal. Bear R on road beside this canal. ◀ Turn L across canal and return to Danube on cycle track along flood dyke. Follow this bearing R alongside Danube on wide cycle track (Dunapart) to **Pünkösdfürdő** (12km, 102m) (accommodation, refreshments).

Bear R following cycle track away from river passing through gap in flood dyke into woods, then continue on riverside cycle track for 3km, passing restaurants, bars, hotels and rowing clubs. Just before railway bridge, turn R where small stream blocks way ahead, then turn L across stream and L again on road down other side. Pass under railway bridge, then follow road (Gázgyár út) away from river between railway R and site of old gasworks L. Bear L around gasworks, which is being developed into high-tech business park called **Graphisoftpark** with tenants including Microsoft and Canon, passing entrance 2. Opposite entrance 1, turn R (Záhony út). and immediately L into Jégtörő út (cycle track R of road) to pass large Auchan supermarket R (16.5km, 104m). ◀

Aquincum, a city of 50,000 inhabitants, was capital of the Roman province of Pannonia. First established about the time of Christ, it reached its heyday in the second and third centuries AD. Among its more notable residents was the future Emperor Hadrian, who was provincial governor at the beginning of the second century. There were two amphitheatres: one civilian and one military, with the latter being larger than the Colosseum in Rome. The city was abandoned early in the fifth century and not rediscovered

Alternative route via cycle track rejoins main route here.

To visit Roman archaeological excavations at Aquincum, continue along Záhony út. Site entrance is on R just before main road.

until 19th-century excavations. At the site, you can see the remains of Roman houses with running water and waste drainage systems; after the Romans left, drainage systems disappeared and did not reappear in Hungary for nearly 1500 years.

Pass a solitary brick chimney stack and, where a wooden fence starts L between cycle track and road, leave cycle track and turn R (Reményi Ede utca) and first L (Leányfalu utca). At T-junction, turn R (Mozaik utca, cycle track R of road) and after 80m follow cycle track across road and continue parallel to railway. By **Filatorigát station**, turn R to cross railway then L to continue on cycle track. Continue ahead beside Ladik utca, parallel with railway, and turn R after disused factory into Bogdáni út. Turn first L (Folyamőr utca) and continue ahead with series of Soviet era residential blocks R. Pass a small car parking area L and bear slightly L, into Laktanya utca. Where this turns more sharply L, continue ahead on cycle track through small park, then on cobbled street (Laktanya utca) to reach T-junction. Turn R into attractive cobbled Fő tér square in **Óbuda** (19km, 107m) (accommodation, refreshments, station).

Aquincum, near Budapest, was a major Roman city

243

Óbuda, nowadays a suburb of Buda, is the oldest part of Budapest. At its heart, Fő tér square has an old town hall and attractive town houses. The town is home to the Imre Varga collection. Born in 1923, Varga is Hungary's leading contemporary sculptor and a number of his works can be seen around Budapest. Óbuda hosts his sculpture of a group of bronze figures, *Women with Umbrellas*.

Keep along L side of square and continue ahead into Szentlélek tér. Cross road ahead and turn L on cycle track beside road parallel with approach road to Árpád hid bridge.

Alternative route via Margitsziget

To visit **Margitsziget**, turn R and L up onto bridge and cross river. After cycling length of island, cross back to main route over next bridge (Margit hid).

Margitsziget today is a car-free 'green lung' for Budapest. Situated between Árpád hid and Margit hid bridges, this 2.5km-long island in the Danube has shady parks, atmospheric ruins, swimming pools, thermal spas and an open-air theatre to attract visitors. King Bela IV (1235–1270) established a Dominican nunnery on the island to educate and look after his daughter Margaret, from whom the island's name is drawn. Later, during the Turkish occupation, the ladies from the pasha's harem were cared for on the island by eunuchs.

For the main route, turn R under bridge and follow cycle track (R of road) past Aquincum Hotel R. Immediately after Timár utca station L, ascend onto combined cycle and pedestrian bridge then turn L over road and railway. Follow cycle track, recrossing main road, and turn immediately L alongside road. Continue between road R and railway L, with iconic skyline of Buda coming into view ahead, to reach Margit hid bridge. ◄

Alternative via Margitsziget rejoins main route here.

Musical fountains on Margitsziget, a popular recreation area for Budapest residents

From here cycle track continues beside road for a final 2km, passing some of Budapest's most famous sights. First pass **Hungarian Parliament** on opposite bank L, then Castle district, **St Matthias church** and **Fishermen's bastion** (partly hidden on hillside R), with old **royal palace** visible beyond next bridge. This ride along Danube ends at W end of city's most famous bridge, **Széchenyi chain bridge**, in centre of **Budapest** (24km, 104m) (accommodation, refreshments, YH, tourist office, cycle shop, station).

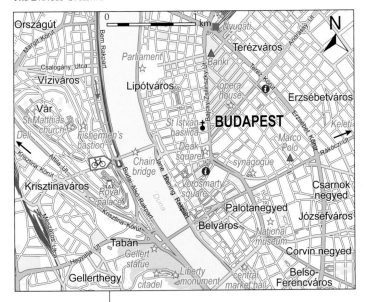

BUDAPEST

In its heyday, Budapest (pop. 1,740,000) was an imperial city with splendour to match that of Vienna. The catastrophe of the Second World War, followed by over 40 years of communism, left the city in a run-down state, with many of its elegant buildings dirty and crumbling. Much work has been done since 1989 to bring the city's architecture back to life, and the freshly cleaned honey-coloured Süttő limestone of Budapest's principal buildings reflects a new optimism in the city.

The current city is a result of the amalgamation in 1872 of Óbuda and Buda – on a hillside west of the Danube – with Pest, on the flat floodplain to the east. Buda had developed as the royal city, first of Hungarian kings and later of Habsburg emperors. The hillside under the old Castle district is riddled with a maze of defensive tunnels. During the Ottoman occupation, the Turkish governor ruled from Buda and fierce fighting during the 1686 liberation left the city in ruins. The houses, churches and buildings of the royal palace complex were mostly built in the 18th century on older foundations, while the citadel was added by Austrian forces to control the city after the 1848 uprising. The most famous landmarks in Buda are St Matthias church and the neighbouring Fishermen's bastion, both of which are in a highly eclectic 19th-century mix of Gothic, neo-classical and art noveau designs known as the Romantic style. Rising behind the Castle district, the Buda hills are an attractive residential suburb and an extensive green lung for the city. A quirky railway operated by children runs through the hills.

Buda is linked to Pest, the commercial and industrial heart of the city, by seven road bridges, all rebuilt after destruction in 1944–1945. The oldest of these, Széchenyi lánchid chain bridge (1849), originally built by British engineers, is a scaled-up version of Marlow bridge, which crosses the Thames in England. Another British-influenced building, the Hungarian Parliament, which is the largest building in Hungary, dominates the riverfront. This was built when the Hungarian government returned to Budapest from Bratislava after 1848. The nearby neo-Gothic St István basilica was completed in 1905. A side chapel contains the hand of St István, the king responsible for introducing Christianity to Hungary. A number of grand boulevards were built in the 19th century. The most famous of these, Andrássy út, which connects Deák Ferenc tér square with *Hősök tere* (Heroes' Square), is lined with classical buildings including the opera house. Beneath the avenue, metro line M1 – the first underground railway in continental Europe (1896) – still retains much of its original appearance.

The Ottoman occupation left its mark via the development of a number of bath houses. The most famous of these, Gellért baths in Buda and Széchenyi baths near Heroes' Square, were massively redeveloped during the 19th and early 20th centuries, with impressive neo-Renaissance buildings being built. Another major influence came from a Jewish population that, pre-Second World War, had reached 250,000. The main synagogue, the largest in Europe, was severely damaged by Nazi supporters and many of its congregation died in concentration camps. Many other Jewish people were rescued by Raoul Wallenberg, a Swedish diplomat. The synagogue was restored in the 1990s with a US$5 million donation from the Estée Lauder foundation and an Imre Varga sculpture of a weeping willow tree, with the names of 400,000 Hungarian victims of the holocaust inscribed on its leaves, stands behind the main building.

Nyugati (western) station was designed by French engineer Gustav Eiffel; while Keleti (eastern) station has statues of engineers Stevenson and Watt adorning its façade.

APPENDIX A
Stage summary table

Stage	Start	Finish	Distance	Waymarking	Page
1	Martinskapelle, Bregquelle (1094m)	Donaueschingen, Donauquelle (678m)	39.5km	Bregtalweg (Furtwangen to Bräunlingen)	45
2	Donaueschingen, Donauquelle (678m)	Tuttlingen, Rathausbrücke bridge (645m)	35.5km	Donau Radweg, Deutsche Donau	53
3	Tuttlingen, Rathausbrücke bridge (645m)	Sigmaringen bridge (571m)	54.5km	Deutsche Donau	60
4	Sigmaringen bridge (571m)	Riedlingen bridge (528m)	33.5km	Deutsche Donau, D6, EV6	67
5	Riedlingen bridge (528m)	Ehingen station (509m)	37.5km	Deutsche Donau, D6, EV6	73
6	Ehingen station (509m)	Ulm, Metzgerturm tower (471m)	41.5km	Deutsche Donau, Albdonaukreis 9	80
7	Ulm, Metzgerturm tower (471m)	Lauingen Marktplatz (441m)	47.5km	Donau Radwanderweg, Deutsche Donau, D6, EV6	89
8	Lauingen Marktplatz (441m)	Donauwörth town hall (408m)	41km	Donau Radwanderweg, Deutsche Donau, D6, EV6	96
9	Donauwörth town hall (408m)	Ingolstadt, footbridge (367m)	59.5km	Donau Radwanderweg, Deutsche Donau, D6, EV6	103
10	Ingolstadt, footbridge (367m)	Kelheim quayside (344m)	50km (45.5km cycling; 4.5km ferry)	Donau Radweg, Deutsche Donau	111
11	Kelheim quayside (344m)	Regensburg, Brückturm (340m)	37.5km	Donau Radweg, Deutsche Donau	119
12	Regensburg, Brückturm (340m)	Straubing, Theresienplatz (337m)	53.5km	Donau Radweg	125
13	Straubing, Theresienplatz (337m)	Deggendorf, Hans-Krämer-Strasse (312m)	39km	Donau Radweg	132

Stage	Start	Finish	Distance	Waymarking	Page
14	Deggendorf, Hans-Krämer-Strasse (312m)	Passau Rathausplatz (301m)	56.5km	Donau Radweg	138
15	Passau Rathausplatz (301m)	Aschach bridge (264m)	65km	Donauradweg R1	147
16	Aschach bridge (264m)	Urfahr, Nibelungen bridge (254m)	26.5km	Donauradweg R1	153
17	Urfahr, Nibelungen bridge (254m)	Mauthausen, Heindlkai (241m)	24.5km	Donauradweg R1	158
18	Mauthausen, Heindlkai (241m)	Grein ferry ramp (240m)	39km	Donauradweg EV6	162
19	Grein ferry ramp (240m)	Melk, Kremser Strasse (209m)	47km	Donauradweg EV6	168
20	Melk, Kremser Strasse (209m)	Krems, Bahnhofplatz (200m)	37.5km	Donauradweg EV6	175
21	Krems, Bahnhofplatz (200m)	Tulln, Nibelungen monument (175m)	44.5km	Donauradweg EV6	183
22	Tulln, Nibelungen monument (175m)	Vienna, Schwedenplatz (164m)	37km	Donauradweg EV6 then Donaukanalradweg after Nussdorf	188
23	Vienna, Schwedenplatz (164m)	Petržalka, Nový Most bridge (142m)	66.5km	Donauradweg EV6	196
24	Petržalka, Nový Most bridge (142m)	Mosonmagyaróvár, Schloss Óvár castle (122m)	37km	Dunajská Cesta (Slovakia), EV6 (Hungary)	208
25	Mosonmagyaróvár, Schloss Óvár castle (122m)	Győr, Széchenyi tér (120m)	40.5km	EV6	213
26	Győr, Széchenyi tér (120m)	Komárom roundabout (113m)	53km	EV6	219
27	Komárom roundabout (113m)	Esztergom basilica (109m)	52.5km	EV6	227
28	Esztergom basilica (109m)	Szentendre, promenade (105m)	48km	EV6 (Eztergom to Nagymaros, Tahitótfalu to Szentendre)	233
29	Szentendre, promenade (105m)	Budapest chain bridge (104m)	24km	EV6	240
		Total distance	**1269km**		

APPENDIX B
Facilities summary table

City/town/village	Stage distance	Cumulative distance	Altitude	Accommodation	Refreshments	YH	Camping	Tourist office	Cycle shop	Station
Stage 1										
Martinskapelle	–	–	1094m	✓	✓					
Furtwangen	7km	7km	862m	✓	✓			✓	✓	
Vöhrenbach	15km	15km	802m	✓	✓			✓		
Hammereisenbach	20.5km	20.5km	755m	✓	✓					
Wolterdingen	28km	28km	718m		✓					
Bräunlingen	34.5km	34.5km	693m	✓	✓		✓	✓	✓	✓
Donaueschingen	39.5km	39.5km	678m	✓	✓			✓	✓	✓
Stage 2										
Pfohren	5.5km	45km	675m		✓		✓			✓
Geisingen	15.5km	55km	667m	✓	✓				✓	✓
Immendingen	23.5km	63km	667m	✓	✓					✓
Möhringen	29km	68.5km	658m	✓	✓		✓	✓		✓
Tuttlingen	35.5km	75km	645m	✓	✓				✓	✓
Stage 3										
Nendingen	5km	80km	637m	✓	✓					✓
Mühlheim	9km	84km	638m	✓	✓					✓
Fridingen	15.5km	90.5km	624m	✓	✓				✓	✓
Beuron	25km	100km	631m	✓	✓					✓
Hausen	33km	108km	598m	✓	✓		✓		✓	
Gutenstein	43.5km	118.5km	591m	✓	✓					
Inzigkofen	50.5km	125.5km	615m	✓	✓	✓				
Sigmaringen	54.5km	129.5km	571m	✓	✓		✓	✓	✓	✓

City/town/village	Stage distance	Cumulative distance	Altitude	Accommodation	Refreshments	YH	Camping	Tourist office	Cycle shop	Station
Stage 4										
Sigmaringendorf	5km	134.5km	567m	✓	✓					✓
Scheer	9km	138.5km	563m	✓	✓					
Mengen	14km	143.5km	561m	✓	✓				✓	✓
Binzwangen	26.5km	156km	538m	✓	✓					
Riedlingen	33.5km	163km	528m	✓	✓		✓	✓		✓
Stage 5										
Zwiefaltendorf	9.5km	172.5km	526m	✓	✓					
Rechtenstein	16km	179km	525m	✓	✓					✓
Untermarchtal	21km	184km	517m	✓				✓		
Munderkingen	25km	188km	516m		✓		✓			✓
Rottenacker	28.5km	191.5km	505m	✓	✓		✓			
Dettingen	34km	197km	494m	✓	✓					
Ehingen	37.5km	200.5km	509m	✓	✓			✓	✓	✓
Stage 6										
Allmendingen	5.5km	206km	515m	✓	✓					✓
Schelklingen	12km	212.5km	534m	✓	✓					✓
Blaubeuren	20km	220.5km	522m	✓	✓	✓		✓	✓	✓
Gerhausen	23km	223.5km	508m		✓					✓
Herrlingen	32km	232.5km	496m	✓	✓					✓
Blaustein	32.5km	233km	496m	✓	✓			✓	✓	✓
Söflingen	37km	237.5km	483m	✓	✓				✓	✓
Ulm	41.5km	242km	471m	✓	✓	✓		✓	✓	✓
Stage 7										
Thalfingen	7km	249km	467m	✓	✓					✓
Oberelchingen	9.5km	251.5km	461m	✓	✓					✓

City/town/village	Stage distance	Cumulative distance	Altitude	Accommodation	Refreshments	YH	Camping	Tourist office	Cycle shop	Station
Unterelchingen	11.5km	253.5km	458m	✓	✓					✓
Weissingen	15km	257km	458m		✓					
Leipheim	20km	262km	452m	✓	✓		✓			✓
Peterswörth	38km	280km	432m	✓	✓					
Gundelfingen	42km	284km	438m	✓	✓					✓
Lauingen	47.5km	289.5km	441m	✓	✓				✓	✓
Stage 8										
Dillingen	6km	295.5km	433m	✓	✓		✓	✓	✓	✓
Steinheim	10.5km	300km	422m		✓					
Höchstädt	13km	302.5km	419m	✓	✓					✓
Sonderheim	17km	306.5km	419m	✓	✓					
Blindheim	19km	308.5km	417m	✓						✓
Gremheim	21.5km	311km	415m	✓						
Zusum	37km	326.5km	401m	✓		✓				
Donauwörth	41km	330.5km	408m	✓	✓			✓	✓	✓
Stage 9										
Zirgesheim	3km	333.5km	400m	✓	✓					
Altisheim	8.5km	339km	413m	✓	✓					
Graisbach	11km	341.5km	407m	✓	✓					
Marxheim	14.5km	345km	402m	✓	✓					
Bertoldsheim	21.5km	352km	397m	✓	✓					
Hatzenhofen	25.5km	356km	389m	✓	✓					
Bittenbrunn	34km	364.5km	386m	✓	✓					
Neuburg	36km	366.5km	384m	✓	✓		✓	✓	✓	
Rohrenfeld	43.5km	374km	378m		✓					✓
Weichering	49km	379.5km	376m	✓	✓		✓	✓		✓
Ingolstadt	59.5km	390km	367m	✓	✓			✓	✓	✓

City/town/village	Stage distance	Cumulative distance	Altitude	Accommodation	Refreshments	YH	Camping	Tourist office	Cycle shop	Station
Stage 10										
Grossmehring	8km	398km	361m	✓	✓					
Vohburg	16.5km	406.5km	356m	✓	✓			✓	✓	
Dünzing	18.5km	408.5km	358m	✓	✓					
Wackerstein	21km	411km	360m		✓					
Neustadt	31km	421km	351m	✓	✓		✓		✓	✓
Bad Gögging	33km	423km	357m	✓	✓			✓	✓	
Weltenburg	45km	435km	349m	✓	✓			✓		
Kelheim	50km	440km	344m	✓	✓	✓		✓	✓	
Stage 11										
Kelheimwinzer	5km	445km	345m	✓	✓					
Poikam	14km	454km	343m							✓
Bad Abbach	17.5km	457.5km	337m	✓	✓					
Oberndorf	19.5km	459.5km	337m	✓	✓					
Matting	24km	464km	338m		✓					
Grossprüfening	31km	471km	335m		✓					
Regensburg	37.5km	477.5km	340m	✓	✓	✓	✓	✓	✓	✓
Stage 12										
Tegernheim	6.5km	484km	329m	✓	✓					
Donaustauf	9.5km	487km	328m	✓	✓			✓		
Frengkofen	18.5km	496km	328m	✓	✓					
Kiefenholz	22km	499.5km	325m		✓					
Pondorf	39km	516.5km	329m		✓					
Kössnach	47.5km	525km	322m	✓	✓					
Sossau	50km	527.5km	318m		✓					
Straubing	53.5km	531km	337m	✓	✓	✓	✓	✓	✓	✓

City/town/village	Stage distance	Cumulative distance	Altitude	Accommodation	Refreshments	YH	Camping	Tourist office	Cycle shop	Station
Stage 13										
Reibersdorf	6km	537km	317m	✓	✓					
Bogen	12km	543km	320m	✓	✓			✓	✓	✓
Pfelling	17km	548km	315m	✓	✓					
Mariaposching	25.5km	556.5km	315m	✓	✓					
Kleinschwarzach	30.5km	561.5km	314m				✓			
Metten	34km	565km	315m	✓	✓			✓		
Deggendorf	39km	570km	312m	✓	✓		✓	✓	✓	✓
Stage 14										
Niederalteich	9.5km	579.5km	314m	✓	✓					
Winzer	17km	587km	314m	✓	✓					
Sattling	21km	591km	306m		✓					
Hofkirchen	24km	594km	306m	✓	✓		✓			
Schmallhof	31.5km	601.5km	301m		✓		✓			
Windorf	35km	605km	303m	✓	✓			✓	✓	
Gaishofen	44km	614km	301m	✓	✓					
Schalding	46.5km	616.5km	301m		✓					
Maierhof	51km	621km	308m		✓					
Passau	56.5km	626.5km	301m	✓	✓	✓	✓	✓	✓	✓
Stage 15										
Pyrawang	13.5km	640km	291m	✓	✓		✓			
Kasten	18km	644.5km	291m	✓	✓		✓			
Engelhartszell	25km	651.5km	283m	✓	✓		✓	✓	✓	
Niederranna	31.5km	658km	287m	✓	✓					
Au	40km	666.5km	276m	✓	✓		✓			
Inzell	43km	669.5km	280m	✓	✓		✓			
Kobling	48km	674.5km	290m	✓	✓					
Kaiserau	58km	684.5km	281m	✓	✓					

City/town/village	Stage distance	Cumulative distance	Altitude	Accommodation	Refreshments	YH	Camping	Tourist office	Cycle shop	Station
Aschach	65km	691.5km	264m	✓	✓			✓	✓	✓
Stage 16										
Brandstatt	3km	694.5km	263m	✓	✓					
Fall	14.5km	706km	265m		✓		✓			
Ottensheim	17km	708.5km	259m	✓	✓		✓	✓		✓
Dürnberg	18.5km	710km	263m		✓					✓
Puchenau	22.5km	714km	269m	✓						✓
Urfahr (Linz)	26.5km	718km	254m	✓	✓	✓		✓	✓	✓
Stage 17										
Pleschingersee lake	4.5km	722.5km	256m				✓			
Abwinden	16km	734km	248m	✓	✓					
Langenstein	21.5km	739.5km	246m	✓	✓					
Mauthausen	24.5km	742.5km	241m	✓	✓			✓	✓	✓
Stage 18										
St Pantaleon	7km	749.5km	241m	✓	✓					
Wallsee	21km	763.5km	233m	✓	✓			✓		
Leitzing	26km	768.5km	229m	✓	✓					
Ardagger-Markt	32km	774.5km	235m	✓	✓		✓		✓	
Grein	39km	781.5km	240m	✓	✓		✓	✓		
Stage 19										
Freyenstein	9.5km	791km	229m	✓	✓					
Willersbach	12km	793.5km	230m	✓	✓		✓			
Donaudorf	17.5km	799km	230m		✓					
Scharlreith	18.5km	800km	227m	✓	✓			✓		
Ybbs	20.5km	802km	217m	✓	✓					✓
Säusenstein	27km	808.5km	217m	✓						✓
Krummnussbaum	31.5km	813km	213m	✓						✓

City/town/village	Stage distance	Cumulative distance	Altitude	Accommodation	Refreshments	YH	Camping	Tourist office	Cycle shop	Station
Pöchlarn	36.5km	818km	213m	✓	✓					✓
Melk	47km	828.5km	209m	✓	✓	✓	✓	✓		✓
Stage 20										
Emmersdorf	4km	832.5km	215m	✓	✓		✓			✓
Aggsbach Markt	11km	839.5km	209m	✓	✓					✓
Groisbach	13.5km	842km	219m	✓						
Willendorf	14.5km	843km	219m	✓	✓					✓
Schwallenbach	16.5km	845km	212m	✓	✓					✓
Spitz	19km	847.5km	206m	✓	✓			✓		✓
St Michael	21.5km	850km	215m	✓	✓					
Wösendorf	23km	851.5km	207m	✓	✓					
Joching	24km	852.5km	202m	✓						
Weissenkirchen	25km	853.5km	207m	✓	✓			✓		✓
Dürnstein	30.5km	859km	221m	✓	✓			✓		✓
Unterloiben	32.5km	861km	214m	✓	✓					✓
Stein	36.5km	865km	198m	✓	✓				✓	✓
Krems	37.5km	866km	200m	✓	✓	✓	✓	✓	✓	✓
Stage 21										
Traismauer marina	17km	883km	187m		✓		✓			
Zwentendorf	31km	897km	179m	✓	✓		✓			
Pischelsdorf	34.5km	900.5km	181m	✓	✓					
Langenschönbichl	37.5km	903.5km	180m	✓	✓					
Tulln	44.5km	910.5km	175m	✓	✓	✓	✓	✓	✓	✓
Stage 22										
Langenlebarn	5km	915.5km	174m	✓	✓					✓
Greifenstein	15km	925.5km	172m	✓	✓				✓	✓
Höflein	17.5km	928km	167m							✓
Kritzendorf	20.5km	931km	169m	✓	✓					✓

City/town/village	Stage distance	Cumulative distance	Altitude	Accommodation	Refreshments	YH	Camping	Tourist office	Cycle shop	Station
Klosterneuburg	24km	934.5km	167m	✓	✓		✓	✓	✓	✓
Kahlenbergerdorf	29km	939.5km	162m	✓	✓			✓		✓
Nussdorf	31km	941.5km	163m		✓				✓	✓
Vienna	37km	947.5km	164m	✓	✓	✓	✓	✓	✓	✓
Stage 23										
Schönau	23.5km	971km	151m		✓					
Orth	30.5km	978km	148m	✓	✓					
Ufer	30.5km	978km	148m		✓					
Eckartsau	37km	984.5km	147m	✓	✓					
Stopfenreuth	43.5km	991km	143m	✓	✓					
Hainburg	50km	997.5km	149m	✓	✓					✓
Wolfsthal	57.5km	1005km	148m	✓	✓			✓		✓
Petržalka (Bratislava)	66.5km	1014km	142m	✓	✓	✓		✓	✓	✓
Stage 24										
Čunovo	17.5km	1031.5km	130m	✓	✓		✓			
Rajka	21km	1035km	130m	✓	✓		✓			✓
Mosonmagyaróvár	37km	1051km	122m	✓	✓			✓	✓	✓
Stage 25										
Halászi	5km	1056km	121m	✓	✓		✓			
Darnózseli	14km	1065km	116m		✓					
Hédervár	17.5km	1068.5km	120m	✓	✓					
Ásványráró	21km	1072km	114m	✓	✓					
Dunaszeg	28.5km	1079.5km	113m	✓	✓					
Győrújfalu	36km	1087km	110m		✓					
Győr	40.5km	1091.5km	120m	✓	✓		✓	✓	✓	✓
Stage 26										
Győrszentiván	8.5km	1100km	113m		✓					✓

257

City/town/village	Stage distance	Cumulative distance	Altitude	Accommodation	Refreshments	YH	Camping	Tourist office	Cycle shop	Station
Bőny	22km	1113.5km	123m		✓					
Bana	26km	1117.5km	126m	✓	✓					
Bábolna	30.5km	1122km	133m	✓	✓					
Ács	40km	1131.5km	117m		✓		✓			✓
Koppánymonostor	47.5km	1139km	120m	✓	✓					
Komárom	53km	1144.5km	113m	✓	✓		✓	✓	✓	✓
Stage 27										
Szőny	4km	1148.5km	111m	✓	✓		✓			✓
Almásfüzitő	11km	1155.5km	110m				✓			✓
Neszmély	18km	1162.5km	117m	✓	✓					✓
Sütő	25.5km	1170km	111m		✓					✓
Lábatlan	29.5km	1174km	118m	✓	✓					✓
Nyergesújfalu	35km	1179.5km	108m		✓					✓
Tát	40.5km	1185km	107m	✓	✓	✓				✓
Esztergom	52.5km	1197km	109m	✓	✓		✓	✓	✓	
Stage 28										
Budbánatvölgy	7km	1204km	109m	✓						
Szob	12.5km	1209.5km	105m		✓					✓
Zebegény	17km	1214km	110m	✓	✓					✓
Visegrád	25.5km	1222.5km	103m	✓	✓		✓	✓	✓	
Dunabogdány	31.5km	1228.5km	103m	✓	✓		✓			
Tahitótfalu	38km	1235km	104m	✓	✓		✓		✓	
Leányfalu	42km	1239km	105m	✓	✓		✓			
Szentendre	48km	1245km	105m	✓	✓		✓	✓		✓
Stage 29										
Pünkösdfürdő	12km	1257km	102m	✓	✓					
Óbuda	19km	1264km	107m	✓	✓			✓	✓	
Budapest	24km	1269km	104m	✓	✓	✓		✓	✓	✓

APPENDIX C
Language glossary

English	German	Hungarian
abbey	Kloster/Stift	kolostor
barrier	Schranke	sorompó
bridge	Brücke	hid
bicycle	Fahrrad	kerékpár/bicikli
castle	Schloss	vár/kastély
cathedral	Dom	katedrális
church	Kirche	templom
cycle track	Radweg	kerékpárút/kerülőút
cyclist	Radfahrer	kerékpáros
dam	Damm	gát
diversion	Umleitung	kitérő út/kerulőut
dyke	Deich	védőgát
ferry	Fähre	komp/rév
field	Feld	mező
floods	Hochwasser	árviz
forest/woods	Wald/Walder	erdő
fort	Festung	erőd
lake	See	tó
monument	Denkmal	műemlék
motorway	Autobahn	autópálya
no entry	Einfahrt verboten	tilos
one way street	Einbahnstrasse	egyirányú utca
puncture	Reifenpanne	defekt
railway	(Eisen)bahn	vasút
river	Fluss	folyó
riverbank	Ufer	folyópart
road closed	Strasse gesperrt	útlezárás
station	Bahnhof	állomás
tourist information office	Fremdenverkehrsbüro	információs iroda
town hall	Rathaus	városháza
youth hostel	Jugendherberge	hostel/ifjúsági szálló

APPENDIX D
Useful contacts

Transportation
SNCF (French railways)
www.oui.sncf

Deutsche Bahn (DB)
0871 8808066 (UK)
+49 180 5996633 (D)
www.bahn.com

Eurostar
0844 8225822
www.eurostar.com

P & O Ferries
08716 642121 (UK)
+44 1304 863000 (outside the UK)
+31 20 2008333 (NL)
www.poferries.com

Stena Line
0844 7707070
www.stenaline.co.uk

European Bike Express
01430 422111
info@bike-express.co.uk
www.bike-express.co.uk

The man in seat 61
(rail travel information)
www.seat61.com

Cycling organisations
Cycle Touring Club (CTC)
0844 7368450
cycling@ctc.org.uk
www.ctc.org.uk

ADFC (German national cycling club)
www.adfc.de

Maps and guides
Bikeline Guides
www.esterbauer.com

Publicpress
www.publicpress.de

Open Street Maps (online mapping)
www.openstreetmap.org

Stanfords
12–14 Long Acre
London
WC2E 9LP
0207 8361321
sales@stanfords.co.uk
www.stanfords.co.uk

The Map Shop
15 High Street
Upton upon Severn
Worcestershire
WR8 0HJ
0800 0854080 or 01684 593146
themapshop@btinternet.com
www.themapshop.co.uk

Accommodation
Youth Hostels Association
0800 0191700
customerservices@yha.org.uk
www.yha.org.uk

Hostelling International (YHA)
www.hihostels.com

Bett+Bike
www.bettundbike.de

Hungarian Tourist Board
(accommodation in Hungary)
www.gotohungary.com

APPENDIX E
Tourist information offices

Germany

Stage 1
Triberg
Wallfahrtstrasse 4, 78098
+49 7722 866490
www.triberg.de

Furtwangen
Lindenstrasse 1, 78120
+49 7723 92950
www.furtwangen.de

Vöhrenbach
Friedrichstrasse 8, 78147
+49 7727 501115
www.voehrenbach.de

Bräunlingen
Kirchstrasse 3, 78199
+49 771 61900
www.braeunlingen.de

Donaueschingen
Karlstrasse 58, 78166
+49 771 857221
www.donaueschingen.de

Stage 2
Tuttlingen
Rathausstrasse 1, 78532
+49 7461 99340
www.tuttlingen.de

Stage 3
Sigmaringen
Schwab Strasse 1, 72488
+49 7571 106224
www.sigmaringen.de

Stage 4
Riedlingen
Marktplatz 1, 88499
+49 7371 1830
www.riedlingen.de

Stage 5
Untermarchtal
Bahnhofstrasse 4, 89617
+49 7393 917383
www.gemeinde-untermarchtal.de

Ehingen
Marktplatz 1, 89584
+49 7391 503216
www.ehingen.de

Stage 6
Blaubeuren
Karlstrasse 2, 89143
+49 7344 96690
www.blaubeuren.de

Blaustein
Bad Blau, Boschstrasse 12, 89134
+49 7304 802162
www.blaustein.de

Ulm
Münsterplatz, Stadthaus, 89073
+49 731 1612830
www.tourismus.ulm.de

Stage 7
Günzburg
Schlossplatz 1, 89312
+49 8221 200444
www.guenzburg.de

Stage 8
Dillingen
Rathaus, Königstrasse 37/38, 89407
+49 9071 52409
www.dillingen-donau.de

Donauwörth
Rathausgasse 1, 86609
+49 906 789151
www.donauwoerth.de

Stage 9
Neuburg
Ottheinrichplatz A 118, 86633
+49 8431 52240
www.neuburg-donau.de

Ingolstadt
Rathausplatz 2 85049
+49 8413 053029
www.ingolstadt-tourismus.de

Stage 10
Vohburg
Donautorgasse 5, 85088
+49 8547 9329869
www.vohburg.de

Bad Gogging
Heiligenstädter Strasse 5, 93333
+49 9445 95750
www.bad-goegging.de

Kelheim
Ludwigplatz 1, 93309
+49 9441 701
www.kelheim.de

Stage 11
Regensburg
Rathausplatz 4, 93047
+49 941 5074410
www.regensburg.de

Stage 12
Donaustauf
Maxstrasse 24, 93093
+49 9403 9552929
www.touristinfo-donaustauf.de

Straubing
Theresienplatz 2, 94315
+49 9421 944307
www.straubing.de

Stage 13
Bogen
Bahnhofstrasse 26, 94327
+49 9422 808855
www.bogen.de

Deggendorf
Oberer Stadtplatz 1, 94469
+49 991 2960535
www.deggendorf.de

Stage 14
Vilshofen
Stadtplatz 27, 94474
+49 8541 208112
www.vilshofen.de

Windorf
Marktplatz 23, 94575
+49 8541 962640
www.markt-windorf-cms.de

Passau (station)
Bahnhofstrasse 28, 94032

Passau (centre)
Rathausplatz 3, 94032
+49 851 955980
www.passau.de

Austria

Stage 15
Engelhartszell
Marktplatz 61, 4090
+43 7717 805516
www.engelhartszell.at

Stage 16
Ottensheim
Marktplatz 7, 4100
+43 7234 8225530
www.tourismus.ottensheim.at

Linz
Hauptplatz 1, 4020
+43 732 70702009
www.linz.at

Stage 17
Mauthausen
Heindlkai 15, 4310
+43 7238 22430
www.mauthausen.info

Stage 18
Wallsee
Marktplatz 2, 3313
+43 7433 2216
www.wallsee-sindelburg.gv.at

Grein
Stadtplatz 5, 4360
+43 7268 7055
www.grein.info

Stage 19
Ybbs
Stauwerkstrasse 86, 3370
+43 7412 55233
www.ybbs.gv.at

Melk
Linzer Strasse 5, 3390
+43 2752 51160
www.melk.gv.at

Stage 20
Spitz
Mittergasse 3a, 3620
+43 2713 2363
www.spitz-wachau.at

Weissenkirchen
Wachaustrasse 242, 3610
+43 2715 2600
www.weissenkirchen-wachau.at

Dürnstein
Dürnstein 132, 3601
+43 2711 200
www.duernstein.at

Krems
Utzstrasse 1, 3500
+43 2732 82676
www.krems.gv.at

Stage 21
Tulln
Minoritenplatz 2, 3430
+43 2272 67566
www.tulln.at

Stage 22
Klosterneuburg
Bahnhof, Niedermarkt 4, 3400
+43 2243 32038
www.klosterneuburg.at

Vienna
Albertinaplatz, 1010
+43 1 24555
www.wien.info

Stage 23
Hainburg
Ungarstrasse 3, 2410
+43 2165 62111
www.feste-hainburg.at

Slovakia

Stage 23
Bratislava
Klobučnicka 2, 81101
+421 216 186
www.bratislava.sk

Hungary

Stage 24
Mosonmagyaróvár
Magyar utca 9, 9200
+36 96 206 304
www.mosonmagyarovar.hu

Stage 25
Győr
Baross Gábor utca 21 (first floor), 9021
+36 96 336 817
www.gyor.hu

Stage 26
Komárom
Igmándi út 2, 2900
+36 34 540 590
www.iranykomarom.hu

Komárno
Župná 5, 94501
+421 773 0063
www.komarno.sk

Stage 28
Visegrád
Duna-Parti út 1, 2025
+36 397 188
www.visitvisegrad.hu

Szentendre
Dumtsa Jenő út 22, 2000
+36 26 317 965
www.iranyszentendre.hu

Stage 29
Budapest
Sütő út 2, 1052
+36 1 438 8080
www.budapestinfo.hu

Budapest
Liszt Ferenc tér 11, 1061
+36 1 322 4098
www.budapestinfo.hu

APPENDIX F
Youth hostels

Germany

Stage 1
Triberg (129 beds)
Rohrbacher Strasse 35, Triberg, 78098
+49 7722 4110

Stage 3
Wildenstein (162 beds)
Leibertingen 88637
(on hillside above Beuron)
+49 7466 411

Sigmaringen (126 beds)
Hohenzollernstrasse 31,
Sigmaringen, 72488
+49 7571 13277

Stage 6
Blaubeuren (114 beds)
Auf dem Rucken 69, Blaubeuren 89143
+49 7344 6444

Ulm (114 beds)
Grimmelfinger Weg 45, Ulm, 89077
+49 731 384455

Stage 7
Günzburg (60 beds)
Schillerstrasse 12, Günzburg 89312
+49 8221 34487

Stage 8
Donauwörth (112 beds)
Goethestrasse 10, Donauwörth, 86609
+49 906 5158

Stage 9
Ingolstadt (84 beds)
Friedhofstrasse 4 1/2, Ingolstadt 85049
+49 841 3051280

Stage 10
Kelheim (103 beds)
Kornblumenweg 1, Ihrlerstein 93346
+49 9441 3309

Stage 11
Regensburg (186 beds)
Wöhrdstrasse 60, Regensburg 93059
+49 941 4662830

Stage 12
Straubing (54 beds)
Friedhofstrasse 12, Straubing 94315
+49 9421 80436

Stage 14
Passau (129 beds)
Oberhaus 125, Passau 94034
+49 851 493780

Austria

Stage 16
Linz (264 beds)
Stranglhofweg 3, Linz 4020
+43 732 664434

Stage 19
Melk (104 beds)
Abt Karl-Strasse 42, Melk 3390
+43 2752 52681

Stage 20
Krems (52 beds)
Ringstrasse 77, Krems 3500
+43 2732 83452

Stage 21
Tulln (126 beds)
Marc Aurel Park 1, Tulln 3430
+43 2272 65165

Stage 22

Vienna (Brigittenau) (306 beds)
Adalbert Stifter Strasse 73, Vienna 1200
+43 1 332 8294

Vienna (Mythengasse) (280 beds)
Mythengasse 7, Vienna 1070
+43 1 5236 3160

Slovakia (all independent hostels)

Stage 23

Bratislava (Downtown) (35 beds)
Panenska 31, Bratislava 81103
+421 2 5464 1191

Bratislava (Patio) (27 beds)
Spitalska 35, Bratislava 81108
+421 2 5292 5797

Bratislava (Possonium) (48 beds
Sancova 20, Bratislava 81104
+421 2 2022 0007

Bratislava (Taurus) (32 beds)
Zámocká 24/26, Bratislava 81101
+421 2 2072 2401

Hungary

Stage 29

Budapest (Aventura)
(near Nyugati station) (25 beds)
Visegradi ut 12, First floor,
Budapest 1132
+36 1 239 0782

Budapest (Banki)
(near Nyugati station) (84 beds)
Podmaniczky ut 8, Budapest 1067
+36 1 413 2555

Budapest (Budapest)
(south-east suburbs) (81 beds)
Könyes Kálmán krt 64, Budapest 1086
+36 1 210 0816

Budapest (Fortuna)
(south-east suburbs) (80 beds)
Gyáli ut 3/B, Budapest 1097
+36 1 215 0660

Budapest (Fortuna boat) (moored
opposite St István park) (89 beds)
Alsó rakpart, Budapest 1137
+36 1 288 8100

Budapest (Grand)
(in Buda hills) (51 beds)
Hűvösvölgyi ut 69, Budapest 1021
+36 1 274 1111

Budapest (Marco Polo)
(near Keleti station) (168 beds)
Nyár ut 6, Budapest 1072
+36 1 413 2555

LISTING OF CICERONE GUIDES

SCOTLAND
Backpacker's Britain:
  Northern Scotland
Ben Nevis and Glen Coe
Cycling in the Hebrides
Great Mountain Days in Scotland
Mountain Biking in Southern and
  Central Scotland
Mountain Biking in West and North
  West Scotland
Not the West Highland Way
Scotland
Scotland's Best Small Mountains
Scotland's Mountain Ridges
Scrambles in Lochaber
The Ayrshire and Arran
  Coastal Paths
The Border Country
The Cape Wrath Trail
The Great Glen Way
The Great Glen Way Map Booklet
The Hebridean Way
The Hebrides
The Isle of Mull
The Isle of Skye
The Skye Trail
The Southern Upland Way
The Speyside Way
The Speyside Way Map Booklet
The West Highland Way
Walking Highland Perthshire
Walking in Scotland's Far North
Walking in the Angus Glens
Walking in the Cairngorms
Walking in the Ochils, Campsie
  Fells and Lomond Hills
Walking in the Pentland Hills
Walking in the Southern Uplands
Walking in Torridon
Walking Loch Lomond and
  the Trossachs
Walking on Arran
Walking on Harris and Lewis
Walking on Rum and the
  Small Isles
Walking on the Orkney and
  Shetland Isles
Walking on Uist and Barra
Walking the Corbetts
  Vol 1 South of the Great Glen
Walking the Corbetts
  Vol 2 North of the Great Glen
Walking the Galloway Hills
Walking the Munros
  Vol 1 – Southern, Central and
  Western Highlands

Walking the Munros
  Vol 2 – Northern Highlands and
  the Cairngorms
West Highland Way Map Booklet
Winter Climbs Ben Nevis and
  Glen Coe
Winter Climbs in the Cairngorms

NORTHERN ENGLAND TRAILS
Hadrian's Wall Path
Hadrian's Wall Path Map Booklet
Pennine Way Map Booklet
The Coast to Coast Map Booklet
The Coast to Coast Walk
The Dales Way
The Dales Way Map Booklet
The Pennine Way

LAKE DISTRICT
Cycling in the Lake District
Great Mountain Days in the
  Lake District
Lake District Winter Climbs
Lake District: High Level and
  Fell Walks
Lake District: Low Level and
  Lake Walks
Mountain Biking in the Lake District
Scrambles in the Lake District
  – North
Scrambles in the Lake District
  – South
Short Walks in Lakeland Books 1–3
The Cumbria Way
Tour of the Lake District
Trail and Fell Running in the
  Lake District

NORTH WEST ENGLAND
AND THE ISLE OF MAN
Cycling the Pennine Bridleway
Cycling the Way of the Roses
Isle of Man Coastal Path
The Lancashire Cycleway
The Lune Valley and Howgills
The Ribble Way
Walking in Cumbria's Eden Valley
Walking in Lancashire
Walking in the Forest of Bowland
  and Pendle
Walking on the Isle of Man
Walking on the West
  Pennine Moors
Walks in Lancashire Witch Country
Walks in Ribble Country
Walks in Silverdale and Arnside

NORTH EAST ENGLAND,
YORKSHIRE DALES AND
PENNINES
Cycling in the Yorkshire Dales
Great Mountain Days in
  the Pennines
Mountain Biking in the
  Yorkshire Dales
South Pennine Walks
St Oswald's Way and
  St Cuthbert's Way
The Cleveland Way and the
  Yorkshire Wolds Way
The Cleveland Way Map Booklet
The North York Moors
The Reivers Way
The Teesdale Way
Walking in County Durham
Walking in Northumberland
Walking in the North Pennines
Walking in the Yorkshire Dales:
  North and East
Walking in the Yorkshire Dales:
  South and West
Walks in Dales Country
Walks in the Yorkshire Dales

WALES AND WELSH BORDERS
Cycling Lôn Las Cymru
Glyndwr's Way
Great Mountain Days in Snowdonia
Hillwalking in Shropshire
Hillwalking in Wales – Vols 1 & 2
Mountain Walking in Snowdonia
Offa's Dyke Map Booklet
Offa's Dyke Path
Pembrokeshire Coast Path
  Map Booklet
Ridges of Snowdonia
Scrambles in Snowdonia
The Ascent of Snowdon
The Ceredigion and Snowdonia
  Coast Paths
The Pembrokeshire Coast Path
The Severn Way
The Snowdonia Way
The Wales Coast Path
The Wye Valley Walk
Walking in Carmarthenshire
Walking in Pembrokeshire
Walking in the Forest of Dean
Walking in the South Wales Valleys
Walking in the Wye Valley
Walking on the Brecon Beacons
Walking on the Gower
Welsh Winter Climbs

For full information on all our
guides, books and eBooks,
visit our website:
www.cicerone.co.uk

Walking – Trekking – Mountaineering – Climbing – Cycling

Over 40 years, Cicerone have built up an outstanding collection of over 300 guides, inspiring all sorts of amazing adventures.

Every guide comes from extensive exploration and research by our expert authors, all with a passion for their subjects. They are frequently praised, endorsed and used by clubs, instructors and outdoor organisations.

All our titles can now be bought as **e-books**, **ePubs** and **Kindle** files and we also have an online magazine – **Cicerone Extra** – with features to help cyclists, climbers, walkers and trekkers choose their next adventure, at home or abroad.

Our website shows any **new information** we've had in since a book was published. Please do let us know if you find anything has changed, so that we can publish the latest details. On our **website** you'll also find great ideas and lots of detailed information about what's inside every guide and you can buy **individual routes** from many of them online.

It's easy to keep in touch with what's going on at Cicerone by getting our monthly **free e-newsletter**, which is full of offers, competitions, up-to-date information and topical articles. You can subscribe on our home page and also follow us on **Facebook** and **Twitter** or dip into our **blog**.

Cicerone – the very best guides for exploring the world.

CICERONE

Juniper House, Murley Moss, Oxenholme Road, Kendal, Cumbria LA9 7RL
Tel: 015395 62069 info@cicerone.co.uk
www.cicerone.co.uk